D1562189

ASIA'S NEW WINGS

THE UNTOLD STORY OF A YOUNG GIRL LOST ON 9/11

ASIA'S NEW WINGS
THE UNTOLD STORY OF A
YOUNG GIRL LOST ON 9/11

CLIFTON & MICHELLE COTTOM

NEXT CENTURY
PUBLISHING

Asia's New Wings: The Untold Story of a Young Girl Lost on 9/11

Published by Next Century Publishing
www.NextCenturyPublishing.com

ISBN: 978-162-9038209

Printed in the United States of America by Versa Press Inc.

ASIA'S NEW WINGS
THE UNTOLD STORY OF A
YOUNG GIRL LOST ON 9/11

Contents

A Masterpiece of a Life

Asia has written a masterpiece with her life. Her profound, yet childlike insights, coupled with the gifted writing skills of many, has made this not just a book with many chapters, but a volume of books about an exciting journey that began somewhere in eternity past and will be read throughout the ages to come. I was, as I am sure you will be, filled with a sense of profoundness and joy while reading of the life of this precious eleven-year-old, for it is neither reactionary nor a careless summary of her purpose for coming to this world "for such a time as this."

Reading Asia's story will grab your attention—and your heart! You will realize the unusual wisdom my granddaughter-in-the-faith had regarding such a sensitive but important subject as this book contains. Her story also invites all people into an intimate relationship with God through the Son.

Asia's life was a learning experience for me; her death, an adventure into the spiritual realm of a loving and sovereign God. As I witnessed her life and her death, many truths about our heavenly Father came to light. I learned, experientially, that our Father does nothing without purpose. As I journeyed into the depths of anger, broken-heartedness, and fear, I eventually came out a better person, with more grace and wisdom. Truly, Asia taught me as much through her death as she did through her life.

This book now puts Asia's life on display for a larger audience to embrace. My hope and prayer is that what her parents and all who love her went through, healed from, and learned will bring comfort and relief to others who travel down the road of loss. Reading and experiencing Asia's story will truly bring healing and life to all those who turn these pages.

Dr. E. A. Ross
Pastor, New Smyrna Missionary Baptist Church
Washington, D. C.

The pain of loss is a part of living, but what determines the degree of pain is the category into which it falls. The loss of a pet is painful, but it's not in the same category as the loss of a child. Not even the loss of your mother or father can compare to the loss of your child. As parents, we can honestly say that the loss of a child is the most grief-filled. No more birthday or Easter celebrations, no Christmas or Halloween parties. Not to mention no graduations, marriages, or new jobs. No grandchildren or christenings, and no "mini" me. No first-time home buyer, no driver's license, no first car ... in fact, there is no life and no more "firsts" at all.

As adults we learn to deal with pain, loss, and death, and we learn to move on. When we have a sick or aging parent, accepting death comes a bit easier. Our District of Columbia Public School (DCPS) kids have coined a phase called "man-up," but how do we really "man-up" when it comes to the loss of a child? Just because death is inevitable, does it mean it's fair in our minds? Does it mean that death is acceptable to our hearts? But more importantly, does "man up" mean we are ready to accept what God allows?

We had to walk this path thirteen years ago. When American Airlines Flight #77 crashed into the Pentagon in Washington D.C., on September 11, 2001, our daughter Asia, only eleven years old, was one of three DCPS students who died on the plane. For days, weeks, and months afterwards, both of us and our son, Isiah, were paralyzed by the darkest grief that one's soul can experience. Dogged by the media, and with no place for solitude, we made our way through with only our family, a few close friends, and each other to lean upon. And we questioned God and our faith, as we often fell asleep asking, "Why?"

As the days turned into weeks, into months, and finally into years, we have come, as a family, to grips with Asia's death. We have truly learned to "man up." And we have learned that God does care; He carries us through our darkest nights and our longest days. We have learned to accept this greatest of loss, the loss of our daughter, and we are now in a different place—a place where we can be used to help others heal. While we don't have answers to why tragedy happens in life, we do have hope that there *is* a tomorrow. And we can offer this hope to others.

Accepting death, loss, and tragedy is no easy pill to swallow. In fact, it can become bitterer the farther down the throat it gets. But all the yelling and screaming, the crying, moaning, and groaning—while they don't negate the reality of accepting what God allows—they are part of the healing process, if we choose to see them this way, instead of succumbing to the bitterness of loss.

This book, *Asia's New Wings*, and the events that led us to write the *Untold Story of a Young Girl Lost on 9/11* offers a sanctuary for those who have experienced or are going through loss and are trying to make sense of it all. Asia's story will give you the strength to endure. It will help you to "go on" and move forward when all your hopes and dreams seem to be over. You may be clutching to a tear-soaked pillow and feel like there is no hope. You may love God with all your heart and soul yet not understand what He's doing or why He allowed your loss. Our daughter's life and story will help you make sense of what you are going through.

Asia's story is about her life and death and how good has grown out of the worst of tragedies. Asia's legacy is one of victory in the time of adversity, including the establishment of the Asia SiVon Cottom (ASC) Memorial Scholarship Fund, a scholarship established for our future leaders and innovators. It's also a story about Asia's family and friends, and how we turned pain and tragedy into healing and learned to go on and live again.

We trust the words you are about to read will help you to gain new strength to face life again. But most of all, we believe this book will show you that God is faithful …

He truly is!

Be Blessed,

Clifton & Michelle Cottom

ACKNOWLEDGEMENTS

From Michelle Cottom

I acknowledge God the Father, my Creator, God the Son, my Lord and Savior, Jesus Christ and especially God, the Holy Spirit, who leads, guides, and directs me into all truths. Thank you for commanding my days.

Second, I acknowledge my immediate family, Cottom and Isiah. Mr. Cottom, I thank you for being my covering, my husband, and my very best friend. There's no way I could have walked through this journey without you, knowing there were a plethora of times when you picked me up and carried me the rest of the way. Talk about "for better or worse"—we've shared the good, the bad, and the ugly. And through it all we are still standing. I bless God for molding and shaping you into the mighty man of God He has called you to be.

Isiah, a prophet you are indeed. Again, I thank God for growing you into the mighty man of God He called you to be. Remember that you can do all things through Christ who strengthens you, and now that you have received the baptism of His Holy Spirit, this is truly your season for greatness. Go forth and make His Name known through all the earth with your lyrics and your lifestyle. Always stay true to God's original intent, and you will never get it wrong.

I acknowledge my Pastor, Bishop Earl A. Ross. There is none like you in all the earth. I thank you, Bishop, for all you have instilled in me. You gave me tools for my journey very early on. I'm not sure if your prophetic anointing foreknew, yet you couldn't tell me, but I thank you because you taught me how to stand when I couldn't feel my legs. You taught me to run and jump because God would give me wings to fly. But most of all you showed me how to accept what God allows whether I like it or not. So calling you my spiritual father doesn't do our relationship justice, but my father—Note Williams—certainly won't mind sharing the title of earthly father with a great man such as yourself.

Apostle Corletta J. Vaughn. I'm not sure words could ever express my gratitude, but let's try this: I'll never forget that if Satan can't stop you from doing the will of God, he'll get in the will of God with you and help you to do it wrong. But most importantly, I'll never ever forget: "Good Morning Holy Spirit" and "Word Wednesday." Everything else with us is due to our kindred spirits and "November 30th."

Last, but certainly not least, I acknowledge, Bishop-Designee Herbert H. Jackson, Jr., my big brother in the Lord. You are my strength, and only God knows that when no one on this side of heaven could help, He stretched forth His hand and sent you. I can NEVER repay you for your loving-kindness. I don't believe anyone on earth knows my heart like you do.

There are so many others in my life that I acknowledge (Pearl, Michael, Mickey Deon, Edie, Paula, Natalie, Erika, Bonnie, Sheila, LaMarsha, Nancy, Stephanie, Castleberry, Gibson, Benson, Bert, Nikki, etc.) but time and space can't hold them all, but please know that I love and appreciate you all.

P.S. I acknowledge America (Mary) Schiavo, the baddest aviation attorney on the planet. Thank you for bringing me closure. Your compassion and integrity is the Armor in my Chain!

ACKNOWLEDGMENTS

From Clifton Cottom

To my loving wife, Michelle, who is my rock, my everything, and the glue that keeps us together. Love you.

To my son, Isiah, who is my hero. He showed me the way to God because, despite all the things he was dealing with, he kept praying. That's my main man for life. LOVE YOU MAN.

Thanks to my mother-in-law, Big Pearl.

Thanks to my Pastor, Bishop Ross.

Thanks to Pastor Herbert Jackson.

Thanks to Benson, Darryl, Anthony, Theo, Bernard and Derek, Gary Washington, John Saunders, Shawn and Vick.

Thanks to my Family.

A special thanks to my mom and dad, Note Williams and Ann Hargrove.

CHAPTER ONE

The Morning of 9/11

"No Mommy, I'm just going to get on the plane and go to sleep."

The last time Clifton and Michelle Cottom saw their eleven-year-old daughter, Asia, was in the family's living room. It was just an ordinary morning of getting ready for work and school, but the family will never forget that day. Her parents were almost as excited as she was. The regular routine of breakfast, baths, and getting dressed was just bit off the everyday rhythm because Asia, Clifton, and her teacher, Ms. Sarah Clark, had to be at Dulles International Airport by 7:00 a.m. Asia's brother, Isiah, slept soundly as his sister quietly, but with a light bounce in her step, made her way around the house getting ready. Asia should have been tired from getting her hair braided until 11:30 p.m., then getting up before dawn, but her enthusiasm for her highly anticipated trip trumped any fatigue. She couldn't believe she was really going!

Asia had been chosen to go on a four-day National Geographic field trip to the Channel Islands National Marine Sanctuary in Santa Barbara, California. The plan was for her to take part in one of America's premier undersea projects—the Sustainable Seas Expedition. It was an incredible honor to be chosen. Ms. Clark had explained that Asia was selected for the trip because she was a good and eager student, she had a bright and energetic personality, and she possessed excellent communication skills. Two other children from the District of Columbia Public Schools (DCPS) were also chosen: Rodney Dickens and Bernard Brown. Their teachers, Mr. James Debeuneure and Ms. Hilda Taylor, accompanied the 6th grade boys. It was truly a once-in-a-lifetime opportunity for the students. Asia, who absolutely loved the water, was ecstatic about her adventure: the trip included long hikes on the beach, kayaking, white water rafting, and marine wildlife monitoring. This trip was much more than just "swimming with the dolphins." It promised to be a uniquely fun-filled and educational experience they would never forget.

In the days leading up to her departure, she asked her parents several questions about the National Geographic Society, its projects, marine biology, and pacific ecosystems. If they were unable to answer her questions, she turned to the Internet to search for the information. That's the kind of girl she was: inquisitive, intelligent, energetic, and full of life.

Asia was most thrilled about being in and on the water on the beautiful Santa Barbara coast. Her enthusiasm was apparent as she grinned from ear to ear whenever she talked about all the things she was going to do.

On the morning of her departure, her mother hugged and kissed her good-bye as she always did and smiled at Clifton who was dropping them off at the airport.

"You stayed up so late last night getting your hair braided; you're going to be tired on the plane," Michelle said to her.

"No Mommy, I'm just going to get on the plane and go to sleep," she replied.

CHAPTER TWO

The Last Drive

"That was her plane. I know it was."

After putting Asia's suitcases in the trunk, Clifton, Ms. Sarah Clark and Asia all got into the car. From the backseat Asia piped up, "Hey, Big Poppa, when I get back we need to do our father-daughter trip."

"Your brother will wanna come. What are you gonna say to him?"

"Don't worry, I'll explain it," she assured her dad.

"You tryin' to be too grown," he said back to her.

"Here's the plan. We'll put the bikes on the truck and go for a ride. Okay, Dad?"

Ms. Sarah Clark laughed and asked Clifton, "What are you going to do with her?" To which he replied, "I'm just gonna spoil her rotten, because if she wanna do it, I'm gonna do it."

Like Father Like Daughter

That's how Clifton treated her. People used to say they were twins because they did everything together, and she looked like Clifton. Asia was an old soul—Clifton always felt as if this wasn't her first time on this earth—

she was too smart for her age.

Clifton hugged and kissed Asia good-bye and then watched her and Ms. Clark pass through those airport doors. It was always hard for him to say good-bye, but Asia knew her dad needed that one last glance of his sweet, exuberant girl. She turned back to smile at him like she always did—not just with her face, but with her entire body.

After Clifton dropped Asia and her teacher off at the airport, he drove to his job as a behavior technician at Asia's school. Traffic was kind of heavy coming from I-66; no surprise there. It was just another day in Washington, DC. The stop-and-go traffic was a nuisance but held an oddly familiar rhythm. Cars ducked in and out of lanes around him, all vying to get to their destinations. To pass the time, Clifton was listening to his usual radio station, the Tom Joyner Morning Show.

He listened halfheartedly, but Tom caught his attention when he interrupted his show to announce that a passenger plane had flown directly into the upper floors of one the Twin Towers, causing a massive explosion and fire. He then announced another passenger plane crashed into the second tower! His thoughts immediately went to Asia. As Clifton drove on, or at least by the time he reached Bertie Backus Middle School (Asia's school), they announced a third plane was missing. He felt as if someone had stabbed him in the heart.

By the time he arrived at the school, students and faculty were panicking. Once inside, he was able to locate his friend Benson and coworker Stacey. He said breathlessly to both of them, "That was my daughter's plane." He couldn't believe he was saying that. His heart was about to burst.

Her Plane

Stacey looked at Clifton strangely. Benson froze. Clifton whispered this time, "That was her plane. I know it was."

It was Clifton's gut feeling, and it was between the Lord and him. Clifton felt as if the two of them were the only ones who knew for sure. He wanted to doubt, but he couldn't. He started to cry.

Stacey was close to Asia because she led the "Steppin'-Up" dance team of which Asia was an honorary member. Stacey put her arm around Clifton and said, "You can't say that now."

Clifton stumbled down to Ms. Clark's empty classroom and stood there stunned. Everything was in its place—books, papers, art materials, pencils, desks, chairs, and bulletin boards. But no Asia or Ms. Clark today. His boss came into the room, took one look at him, and said, "Go home, we got this."

Michelle called Clifton while he was heading out of the building. "Hey, did you hear what happened?"

"Yeah."

"What flight was Asia on?" Michelle asked.

"I don't know." His heart sank. He couldn't tell his wife his worst fears.

"I'm headed home," she said.

"Me too."

Clifton pushed his way through the parents scrambling to get their kids from the school. It was chaos. He drove the short distance to his house and found it full of friends and family.

CHAPTER THREE

A Mother's Fears

"I have to find out if she is safe."

On September 11, 2001, Michelle was at work at the United States Department of Agriculture (USDA) in Washington, DC. That day she was the acting director for the Agricultural Marketing Service Civil Rights Program because her director was leading a training seminar out of the building. She was conducting official business with one of the contract attorneys. They were discussing the strengths and weaknesses of a case of employment discrimination that was soon to come to trial before the US Equal Employment Opportunity Commission. Everyone was so busy working that they had no idea anything was going on in New York. It was just another day at the office.

Michelle was in the midst of that conference call when all of a sudden LaKeisha, the office secretary, came in with a look of horror on her face. "Michelle, come look: a plane just crashed into one of the Twin Towers!"

They watched in disbelief as fire and smoke consumed the upper portion of the North Tower of the World Trade Center in New York. The streets were filled with frantic, screaming people. More USDA employees joined the two women as they stood watching the television with their hands over their mouths. Then a second plane crashed into the South Tower. The crowd let out a collective gasp. Both buildings were burning: It looked like a scene from a horror movie.

Where is My Child?

Although Michelle remained outwardly calm—likely attributable to her military training—her immediate thoughts and concerns went to Asia. "My child is on a plane somewhere headed to California," she said to those around her. "I have to find out if she is safe."

Michelle's entire office, and the attorney involved in the conference call, peppered her with questions about Asia and her flight as they all frantically searched for information on her whereabouts. Michelle called the principal of Asia's school to ask him what flight she was on, but he could not tell her. As a woman of faith, it never entered her mind that Asia was dead. However, she grew increasingly concerned because she didn't know where Asia was, so she prayed silently, *Lord, please keep her safe.*

Everything around Michelle was in utter turmoil. Like New York City, Washington D.C. was also in a state of panic due to the attack. The US government acted quickly to contain and control the massive damage and prevent further loss of life by ordering the immediate evacuation of all federal buildings in D.C.

The cell towers were understandably flooded with calls from worried parents, children, friends, and colleagues, and the sheer volume overwhelmed the system causing the towers to malfunction. Fortunately, Michelle's cell phone carrier still had service, so her mobile phone was working for a little while. Michelle phoned Clifton and asked him if he knew Asia's flight number. He couldn't or wouldn't tell her. Later on she found out he had known, but he didn't want to tell her because he didn't want to admit it to himself that the worst had happened.

Even amidst the terror and confusion of the ordeal, hearing Clifton's voice grounded Michelle for a moment. She really wanted to phone *anyone* to find out where her daughter was, and the agony of her inability to communicate with anyone was excruciating.

It was time to evacuate the building. Michelle instructed everyone to go home, and then she left. Asia's school was just around the corner from their house, so she hoped to find some answers there.

Chaos and Confusion

Adding to the commotion, the evacuation of thousands of people was cumbersome. With police lines everywhere, the city seemed to be quarantined. Traffic was closed around every federal building and streets leading into and out of the Pentagon. (The Pentagon is just across the Potomac River from the USDA.) Once outside, Michelle heard the screams of sirens—hundreds and thousands of them. People poured into the streets as government buildings closed one by one. It felt as if the city were under attack as everyone rushed to the subways to get out of the capital.

As she boarded the overcrowded train, someone must have given her a seat, but Michelle never noticed who it was. *Where is Asia?* She breathed out the words as the train lumbered slowly out of the station and into the daylight. She called Pearl, her mother, and asked her to pick her up from the subway station.

The D.C. Metro is much like a surface train except it has very large windows for the tourists. As the train pulled out of the station, it came above ground. Through windows meant to better appreciate the grandeur and plentiful historical sites of the city, Michelle stared at black smoke rising upwards into the sky, not knowing at that moment that the smoke was coming from the Pentagon. Nor did she realize that it was Asia's plane, Flight #77, that had crashed into the Pentagon. Pearl picked her up from the subway station and drove the short distance to Michelle's house. When Michelle walked in and saw the look of agonized worry on Clifton's face, her heart sank.

Everything quickly turned to total mayhem as friends and family arrived. By this time, everyone knew that Asia was missing. Michelle immediately went to the phones and was frantically trying to locate Asia's plane. She was calling everywhere: the school, the National Geographic Society, and the hotel in Santa Barbara, California, to see if the kids had arrived, but the flight hadn't landed at that time, no one knew for certain if Asia was on one of the doomed planes. The *not knowing* was almost unbearable.

CHAPTER FOUR

Lives Forever Changed

"Not my will but your will be done."

The television reporters kept saying Flight #77 was missing, but they also reported that a plane had crashed into the Pentagon. Michelle asked herself, "How does a plane go missing in this day and age?" Something was terribly wrong. At about 11:40 a.m. the news channels initially reported an explosion at the Pentagon. Then it was reported that a plane had hit the Pentagon, but there was no confirmation it was Flight #77. Michelle felt her stomach sink as her greatest fear seemed to be coming true.

"That's her plane; it hit the Pentagon ... I just know it in my heart," Pearl screamed at Michelle.

"Don't say that. Where is your faith?" she replied, holding out hope that Asia would be one of the survivors.

An Inconsolable Father

Michelle watched Clifton trudge up the stairs, and then asked Pearl to check on him. Suddenly, she heard Clifton screaming, and she ran up the steps only to see Pearl trying to hold him back. He pushed past her and ran down the steps screaming that he was going to the Pentagon to get his child. Friends finally stopped him in the yard and tried to console him, but he was inconsolable. When Michelle came back downstairs, she collapsed onto the dining room table and quietly prayed, "Nevertheless Lord, not my will but Your will be done."

The collage of emotions inside the house added more confusion. Some friends and family tried to comfort her by saying that she shouldn't worry—maybe Asia wasn't on that plane, and maybe it would be just a matter of time before everyone found out it was all merely a nightmare.

Someone decided to turn off the television to shield the family from the horror of the unfolding events. They didn't see the people jumping out of buildings in New York, for which the Cottoms are thankful; they had enough to deal with. Later, much later, the family learned that some of them plunged to death on their own, others jumped in groups, and two people were holding hands on the way down.

The family also didn't see the news reports showing the South Tower collapsing to the ground in free fall and the dust and debris that enveloped the streets. Nor did they see that 45 minutes after the South Tower collapsed, the North Tower fell in the same way. In the Cottom house, there was panic and agitation; they did not know how to deal with their fear or how to comfort each other.

A Brother's Sorrow

Isiah came home from school on the bus, as usual, but with the unusually heavy traffic, it took him five hours to get there. When he got home, he saw everyone in front of his house and he thought, *We are having a party*. He didn't know what was going on.

By this time, Clifton had calmed down. Heavy-footed, he made his way over to Michelle, put his hand on her shoulder, and whispered in her ear, "We gotta tell him before he hears it from someone else."

Michelle called Isiah over, then put her arm around him and said, "Come on upstairs. Your dad and I need to talk to you." As they made their way through the crowded room and up the stairs, Michelle tried to shield Isiah's eyes from the friends and family who were visibly panicking, but that was an impossible task. *How are we going to tell him? Should we give him hope? We still haven't heard if there were any survivors. No, we can't give him false hope. Isiah, how will you handle this? Your sister. Your best friend.*

By this time, Isiah knew something was desperately wrong. The three of them walked into Clifton's and Michelle's bedroom, and sat down on the bed. Michelle began to speak. "It looks like Asia was on a plane that was hijacked and crashed into the Pentagon."

Isiah said, "I don't want to hear no more." He screamed, then he covered his face with his hands and fell to his knees and prayed. Clifton and Michelle stayed with him for a while, not knowing how to comfort him when they couldn't even console themselves.

Official Confirmation

Later that night the news reporter announced, "It is officially confirmed that American Airlines Flight #77 has hit the Pentagon." Then a list of the names of all the passengers scrolled onto the TV screen, including Asia Cottom. With sinking hearts, Clifton and Michelle knew their world was forever changed.

CHAPTER FIVE

Here Only a Short Time

"They ran my baby's plane into a building."

Later that night, after everyone but a few close relatives had left, Clifton went down to the basement, and Michelle went to check on Isiah. Both Isiah and his cousin, Mike, were now sound asleep, still wearing their school clothes. Michelle didn't want to disturb them.

Never Okay Again

When Michelle made it back to her bedroom and collapsed onto the bed, she felt so exhausted, but she couldn't sleep. She called her grandmother in Ohio, whom she calls Ma, to see if she was okay. Michelle knew she wouldn't be, nor would she ever be again. Ma was crying in disbelief. Earlier that day, Michelle had called her god-sister, Nancy, to deliver the devastating news and to ask her to please drive over to Ma's house and tell her in person what had happened. Both Nancy and her husband, Gene, were especially close to the family. In fact, they were next-door neighbors throughout Michelle's entire childhood. Asia often stayed overnight with them when she was visiting her great-grandmother, and she enjoyed spending time with Nancy's two daughters. Nancy and Gene were still with Ma when Michelle called.

They talked for a while, but then Ma said she wasn't feeling very well. Neither was Michelle! Ma assured her she would come as soon as she could.

Michelle doesn't remember if or when Clifton came to bed the night of 9/11. The next day, another influx of people came to the house. The news reporters must have gotten wind of the fact that it was the Cottoms' daughter on one of the planes, so they camped outside the house. They tried to get into their home, and some of them tried to sneak in with the people bringing food. They acted as if they were friends and family, but as soon as they were inside they asked questions and took pictures and put microphones in their faces. The guests had to physically remove the intruders from the house.

The FBI

It was around noon when the FBI agents rang the doorbell. Clifton opened the door to the sight of two officers, one male and one visibly pregnant female. She said, "It is with deep regret we have come to inform you that it is confirmed that indeed Flight #77 hit the Pentagon, and there were no survivors."

Michelle didn't say anything. She couldn't talk to her. Michelle stared at the FBI's bulging abdomen. Michelle became enraged that the government could be so insensitive as to send a pregnant woman to give a grieving mother this devastating news. The agent clearly read Michelle's facial expression, so she began to apologize. Michelle walked away and let Clifton handle the matter. Clifton thought to himself, *That's evil at work. Why in the world would the FBI send a pregnant agent to tell my wife that she had just lost her daughter? That's the last thing Michelle needs to see right now.* He and Pearl escorted the agents out the door.

Michelle still wonders, *Don't they have protocol for who should tell someone their loved one has passed and how to do it?*

Two days later, Michelle's oldest brother, Michael, arrived from Germany. He is affectionately referred to as "Military Mike" because he is ex-military, an armed cavalry scout, who used to ride on the tops of tanks while on active duty. He is the toughest person Michelle knows, and yet he appeared visibly shaken when he finally reached her. Although flights were shut down everywhere, American Airlines was able to get him home quickly on a commercial business class flight.

He came through the door, and Michelle fell into his arms and said to him, "They ran my baby's plane into a building."

He hugged her and said, "I know, yeah Sis, I know."

Family Comforting Family

Then Mike drove to Ohio to pick up Ma and bring her to them because she was afraid to fly. Six days after 9/11, Michelle's ma finally arrived. Michelle didn't sleep until her ma was safely in the home. At night Ma sat on the end of Michelle's bed to comfort her, just as she often did when Michelle was a child, and that is how Michelle was finally able to go to sleep.

Because Michelle's grandmother had raised her, she always considered her to be her mom. Asia loved her too. When Asia came home from school, the first thing she would do every day was call her great-grandmother in Ohio, and they would talk for hours. Asia would stay with her whenever she could. Ma taught Asia the same things she had taught Michelle growing up such as how to be a lady, how to walk in 1/2 inch wedge heels, and how to show respect to one's elders, others, and to oneself.

Michelle's grandmother often said, "Asia does everything fast. She is always moving." Later, after Asia passed, Ma solemnly added, "It's as if she knew she would only be here for a short while."

In the days, weeks, and months following 9/11, Ma sat for hours on the front porch of her house and stared off into the distance while all the commotion of the traffic blared around her. It was like she was giving up the will to live. One reporter interviewed her and Ma said in a subdued voice, "I never did like flying. I will never fly again." Seventeen months later, she developed pancreatic cancer and died within a short time. Michelle thinks Ma knew about her cancer for a long time but didn't want to burden anyone. That's the kind of person she was. It gave Michelle great comfort that Asia's beloved great-grandmother joined her in heaven, but, now Michelle had lost her daughter and "mother" in less than two years.

CHAPTER SIX

Hate is Never the Answer

"Why did they do this, God?"

Michelle and Clifton were mourning the loss of their child at the same time the nation was mourning the loss of close to 3,000 lives.

It is excruciatingly painful to lose a child, especially in a senseless act of violence. Asia wasn't ill or doing anything wrong.

Eight children in total died during the 9/11 attacks. Unlike Asia and the two boys traveling with their teachers on American Airlines Flight #77, the other five children all had one or both parents with them. Dana and Zoe Falkenberg were on the same flight as Asia, and they were three and eight years old at the time. Juliana McCourt was four, David Gamboa-Brandhorst was three, and Christine Hanson was two. They were all traveling on United Airlines Flight #175 when it crashed into the South Tower of the World Trade Center. All those children were taken before they were even teenagers. No sweet 16. No graduation. No marriages. No careers. No children.

A Place of Acceptance

Just like many American families, the Cottoms were living the American Dream before 9/11, vacationing every year in kid-friendly places like Disney World, Cedar Point, Six Flags of America and Hershey Park. After 9/11, Michelle and Clifton thought they would never come to peace with this tragedy that had befallen their family and the nation. Michelle can honestly say that it has taken her thirteen years to finally accept what God allows, whether she likes it or not. Despite ongoing pain, they have come to a place of acceptance.

In the days and weeks that followed 9/11, some people immediately turned to hatred. Yes, the Cottoms were angry with God, but they chose not to hate an entire race of people. That is just not what their family is about. Hate is taught. They don't have anything against the people from those countries. As far as they know, the people who killed Asia died on that plane along with her. Why would they hate everyone who looks like them? It's just like they can't hate all Caucasians because certain white people behaved atrociously during the time of slavery. They don't have any reason to hate these people unless they were *taught* to hate them. No one comes out of the womb hating others.

Teach the Children

If children are taught—though some of them may go astray—correctly at home, then the words of Proverbs 22:6 can be trusted: "Train up a child in the way he should go, and when he is old he will not depart from it." Michelle and Clifton believe that is applicable for all parents who are raising children, regardless of the type of faith one has or even the absence of faith. If you train children—or teach children—in the way that they should go, they won't hate. Love is the natural instinct. Everyone comes out of the womb loving others. Clifton and Michelle refuse to participate in the hatred that came out of 9/11.

CHAPTER SEVEN

A Loving Family

"Hey man, come on over here."

It was mainly Clifton's love and protection that helped Michelle through this ordeal. She says he's a real man, caring first and foremost for his family. He'll tell you that it was Michelle's love that carried him through. They both held each other up and supported each other, and never left each other, not even for a day, no matter how tough the battle became. They had different ways of dealing with their pain because they are different people, but that doesn't matter. What does matter is that they always supported and loved each other, and they still do.

So Much Alike

Michelle still remembers the day when she first met Clifton. Her brother Greg invited Isiah and her to a July 4th cookout that Clifton was hosting. Greg and Clifton were best friends, and they did almost everything together. They grew up playing basketball on the streets of Washington, DC. Clifton's family treated Greg like one of their own. Greg and Michelle's mother, Pearl, often said that Clifton and Michelle should meet because they are so much alike. *If your brother and your mother are*

47 | P a g e

recommending a certain guy, he must be all right, Michelle remembers thinking.

When Isiah was young, his father and Michelle separated. She had left the military by then, so the two of them moved back home to Ohio to be with Michelle's grandmother and to start a life anew.

Isiah's Rough Start

Isiah had a rough start to his life. He was born three months premature with hydrocephalus (water on the brain), and a larger-than-normal soft spot. Like many preemies, he was so premature that his lungs were underdeveloped, requiring him to remain in an incubator for quite some time. He was born in the early 1980s, so medical care wasn't as sophisticated as it is nowadays. The usual procedure would be to put a shunt in his ear to drain the fluid from the brain, but because they were trying to keep him alive, they chose not to do that at that time, so the water stayed on his brain longer than it should have. Because of this, he was diagnosed as mildly delayed in some respects. However, it's hard to notice now, and his creative mind more than makes up for it. At the cookout, Clifton saw Michelle carrying Isiah around, so he asked her, "Why you holdin' that big ol' boy?" Michelle told him that it's because he can't walk. Isiah never even crawled; he just scooted on his buttocks.

"Sure he can walk. How old is he?" he asked.

"Two," she replied.

"You just have to put him down and he'll walk, if he wants to."

She tried to stand Isiah up, and he just flopped down on his butt.

Clifton kept saying to Isiah, "Come on, come on here." Isiah was laughing and grinning—clearly enjoying the attention he was getting—but he wouldn't walk.

Clifton dug into his own pocket and pulled out a five-dollar bill and said, "Hey man, come on over here." Michelle stood Isiah up again, and he walked to him, and they have been thick as thieves ever since.

"What money can do," Clifton said with a grin.

After her divorce was finalized, Clifton and Michelle started dating on and off.

It was at that time the automobile industry began to deteriorate, which turned Ohio sideways; finding and keeping a good job was next to impossible. Michelle's experience in the military wasn't really considered relevant work experience for most jobs in Ohio, so she went back to business school. She was also looking for suitable employment.

Moving to Washington

Michelle's brother Greg wanted to help her out. He asked, "Why don't you come live here in Washington with me and work for the government?" Michelle has always been close to her brothers, so Isiah and Michelle packed up their apartment and relocated to D.C. She also has many relatives in D.C. because that is where she was born. Another factor swaying her decision to move back home was because Washington D.C. has excellent schools for children with learning disabilities, so she knew Isiah would be better off. Also, she would be closer to Clifton.

So, Clifton and Michelle kept dating. Eventually she got pregnant with Asia, and they got married.

When the kids were young, Clifton would drill Asia and Isiah on the way home from church. "What did he preach about?" They would say they listened to the preacher because they knew he was going to ask about it.

Isiah Today

Isiah recently turned thirty years old. He works in the food and nutrition services at the VA Medical Center, and he writes and performs rap music. His music appeals to all people whether they believe in God or not. There is no specific category his music falls into. He is a music lover of what is called "ol' school rap," such as The Sugar Hill Gang, Curtis Blow, Run DMC, Heavy D, Doug E Fresh, Will Smith, and LL Cool J type rappers. He also loves some of the new artists like LeCrae and Trip Lee.

Isiah struggled mightily with the loss of his sister. Sure, they used to fight like all siblings do, but her loss still affects him today.

Michelle often tells Isiah that he shouldn't be limited by what people think and what they say about him. He may not be as articulate sometimes as he would like to be, but his intelligence and grace truly amazes his parents.

Recently Isiah has been diagnosed with epilepsy. For some reason, he only started having seizures within the last five years. Even the stress of Asia's death didn't trigger them. Now he has to make sure he gets adequate daily rest and consistent medication to prevent them. During the past eighteen months, his seizures have been out of control. He was having three or four of them every six weeks. The National Institute of Health has put him in a seizure study, among other things, and his doctors are adjusting his medication as best they can to keep his blood levels right. His parents think his recent treatment is working. They are putting their trust in God!

CHAPTER EIGHT

Healing Takes Time

"This is all I have left of Asia"

As much as we talk about our children, and love them so dearly, they aren't ours to keep. Michelle says that she and Clifton were blessed to have Asia, but she was on loan. Michelle thought it was a long-term loan; little did they know that the lifetime would only last eleven years.

Limitation, Talents, and Gifts

We all have limitations, talents, and gifts. If it weren't for Clifton, Michelle said she would struggle with balancing the checkbook and staying on their monthly budget. He may not be the faster reader, but math and accounting are his thing. He helps Michelle fill out their tax forms every year, and he is often tutoring people in math. Clifton's and Michelle's running joke is Asia's godmother, La Marsha, owes part of her B.A. to Clifton for helping her through her college math classes.

Initially, Clifton didn't know how to deal with the loss of Asia. He thought he had to be strong. In his mind, being strong meant he shouldn't show his emotions. How does one prepare oneself to hear the news that hijackers took over your daughter's plane and smashed it into a building? In America, no one is taught how to deal with that type of horror. There are no textbooks or classes. When it happens you have to start the healing process the best way you know how.

Clifton put up a good pretense for a while. But Michelle knew he was struggling when he started to do some crazy, crazy things. He explains them in his words later on, but one of the most troubling episodes for Michelle was when they received a memento from the Pentagon.

One night, Michelle came home from school very late and all the lights were off in the house and outside. No porch light, not anything. This was very unusual because Clifton *always* left the lights on for her safety. Clifton has always been a very good husband and very protective of her. His mother taught him well. When Michelle pulled in the drive and opened the garage, both of his cars were there so Michelle said to herself, *He must be knocked out asleep and has been for some time. I can't believe he didn't leave the lights on.*

As she entered the house with all her bags there was an eerie quietness. Even the house alarm wasn't on. She turned on the alarm and proceeded to put down her bags and look for Clifton to find out why the house was dark. She went to their bedroom, no Clifton; she went to the basement, no Clifton; she looked out back and a few other places, but no Clifton. By this time she assumed he wasn't home. Then she heard a sound like a wounded animal. As she followed the sound, much to her shock, she found him curled up on the floor of his closet in the fetal position with a red, white, and blue cloth covering him and crying hysterically.

"What's wrong? What is this?" Michelle demanded. He couldn't speak; he just sobbed.

Michelle picked up a box that was on the floor beside him. It was a FedEx box from the Pentagon. Inside she found a letter explaining that the cloth Clifton was wrapped in was the cover that adorned Asia's bench at the Pentagon. Because they did not attend the dedication ceremony, the bench cover was mailed to them.

All That is Left

Finally, Clifton looked up at Michelle and said, "This is all I have left of Asia, my only child." He also said some other pretty ugly, hateful things, but Michelle knew it was his grief talking, and therefore doesn't wish to repeat it. She had no idea that after all this time, ten years after her death, Clifton's pain and loss were still so deep inside him. She was absolutely stunned. She never saw him display such raw emotion.

Michelle was in the middle of her counseling classes and had read a few textbooks about grief but nothing could prepare her for the deep pain Clifton had finally let out. This was the first time she realized that this pain would be part of their lives forever. How were they ever going to be able to move on? How could Michelle, as a wife, now help her husband?

This was a true test of faith and their marriage. She knew at that point they had to get him some help in healing.

CHAPTER NINE

No Ordinary Child

"I'm going to be eleven forever."

Asia was no ordinary child. She truly lived her life in "double time," as if she knew she wouldn't be long here on earth. You could say she fit more into her eleven years than most people do in twenty-two! She was a large, healthy baby, weighing in at 9lbs 15 1/2 ounces at birth. She was Clifton's only biological child.

Michelle has always loved the name Asia. When she was pregnant with Isiah, she chose two names, Isiah or Asia, depending upon whether the baby was a boy or a girl. She liked the name Asia for a girl and kept it in mind for when or if she had a daughter.

Active Asia

As Asia became a toddler, she crawled only briefly—so briefly that Michelle can't even remember—because she started walking early, at nine months of age. Asia was an extremely active child. She loved bowling, dancing, putt-putt golf, swimming, jumping rope, biking, skating, rollerblading, and soccer. The year she died, she wanted Michelle to teach her and her brother tennis, but they never got the chance to before Asia passed away. Asia also enjoyed typical American food such as

McDonalds, pizza, french fries and chicken wings. (She used to call chicken wings "triangles" because that's what they look like. Isiah said that if he ever opens a restaurant, he will call it "Triangles." Everything in the restaurant will be shaped in a triangle. A sandwich would be cut into triangles, for example. Michelle is sure he will work out all those details on this.) Asia also loved all the girly-girl things such as nail polish, dresses, purses, lip gloss, perfume, jewelry, Barbie dolls, and Tweety Bird.

It was Michelle's grandmother who taught Asia how to bake and cook, how to make ice cream out of snow, and create donut holes, Jell-O, and Kool-Aid squares.

Asia was absolutely smitten with babies. She and her friend, Natalie Washington, played with them in the church whenever they could, and those same little ones sat with Asia and Natalie during the church services as soon as they were old enough.

Michelle's girlfriend Sheila delivered her baby, Dominique, in the latter part of August 2001. Asia desperately wanted to see Dominique before she left for her school trip. She hugged and hugged that little baby during her last visit. Dominique is now thirteen years old, and Sheila and Michelle often say that she reminds them so much of Asia, just her mannerisms and the things she says and does. Dominique and Isiah fight all the time, just as Asia did. Isiah calls Dominique his new little sister.

The other baby Asia adored is Michelle's cousin's daughter Jasmine, who also misses Asia terribly. Whenever Michelle babysat Jasmine, Asia would give her a bath, put her lotion on, and then dress her. Jasmine followed Asia around the house, wanting to do everything Asia did.

While Clifton and Michelle appreciated Asia's love for babies, they wanted her to grow tired of them so that when she was older she wouldn't have one too soon. Michelle used to warn her, "It's okay to love babies, Asia, but you shouldn't want one until it is really your time."

School Days

Asia attended Bunker Hill Elementary School from kindergarten through the 5th grade. She transitioned to Bertie Backus Middle School for her 6th grade, just shortly before she died. One of her first assignments at her new school was to fill in her Student/Parent Handbook for the 2001-2002 school year. She included all of her personal information, plus she listed her best friends as Natalie and her brother Isiah, and her parents as her heroes. Michelle was surprised, and laughed, that Asia had chosen her as one of her favorite singers. While Michelle can hold a note, she certainly doesn't think of herself as a great singer. They still cherish that notebook to this day. It was one of her last written messages to them.

All Asia knew was school, family, and God. Her faith was at the core of who she was. While most children read condensed and simplified children's versions of the Bible, and they latch onto easy-to-understand Bible verses, not Asia. She was serious about her faith in God, and her favorite Bible verses were complicated. Her favorite Bible verse was Revelations 21:8.

Asia was plucked from this earth just as she was starting to bloom, not only spiritually, but also physically. She was a girl barely beginning the transition into womanhood.

On the Cusp of Womanhood

A few days before the trip, Asia was riding her bicycle on her street with some friends from the neighborhood. She had taught herself to ride a two-wheeler before others her age. She and Isiah used to ride around their neighborhood to go to the nearby park. If the weather was bad, they would ride in the basement, sometimes with their neighborhood friends. They were a tight group who played together every day; usually they played Double Dutch or hide-and-go-seek.

One day when she was riding her bicycle on their front sidewalk, she took the corner too sharply and wound up falling hard onto the pavement. She ran inside the house crying from the pain. Michelle helped her clean and dress the scrape on her knee. A little while later, she went to the bathroom and came out with a look of terror on her face. "Mommy, I am still bleeding from my fall." As it turned out, it was her very first menstrual cycle. Michelle asked her to come and join her in her bedroom.

Asia's bunk beds were covered with her Barbie comforter sets. Stuffed toys and dolls adorned the top bunk. Tweety Bird was emblazoned on toys, clothes, books, and pictures. She had her large Barbie Dream House on the table in her room. Barbies were in the closets and everywhere else in her room, all of them with that perpetual smile. Asia moved one of the Barbies in the Dream House from the living room couch to the elevator.

Michelle patted the comforter to encourage Asia to sit beside her on the bed. As soon as she joined Michelle, she put her arm around her and looked at her lovely smiling face for a moment. *She's too young to have to deal with this; she's still a child.* But Michelle took a deep breath and then explained the purpose of the womanly cycle, and what was involved.

"E-w-w-w, that's nasty Ma. Every month? For how long?"

Michelle said, "It depends; some women have it for three days, some have it for seven ..."

"Oh, my God!"

The next day, Michelle took the day off work, and Asia stayed home from school so they could spend a quality mother-daughter day together. Her daddy went to work, and Isiah was off to school, so Asia and her mom enjoyed a leisurely breakfast then went shopping. Of course, it's always special to a child if the mother takes a day off from the office, especially in their situation, because Michelle often travelled for her work.

They talked more about the transition, and the birds and the bees, and then they shopped for feminine products. Asia found the hygiene section in the store, and then she held up a box of tampons and yelled—she was loud, just like Clifton—down the aisle to Michelle, "Hey Ma is this what goes up your butt?"

Two female shoppers howled with laughter, and

one of them asked, "First period?" Michelle turned fifty shades of red.

Later that day Asia asked incredulously, "Grandma in Ohio has a menstrual cycle?"

"She used to have one," Michelle replied. "Yes, Asia, *all* women have them."

Asia couldn't believe her beloved great grandma could have something so foul.

"Well, *I* am only going to have *one* of these."

"Oh no, you are going to have one every month," Michelle replied, laughing.

"No, I'm only going to have *one* of these." She crossed her arms and scowled.

Michelle thought Asia was just protesting, and it was her way of refusing to accept what is natural to all women. In hindsight Michelle wonders if this was a prophetic moment of her just *knowing*.

Michelle still looks back on that time, of her transitioning into womanhood, and she cherishes the memories of that day.

Never Going to Grow Up

Another moment that may be seen as prophetic is that on the Sunday before her trip she was sitting in church with Pearl and Michelle's sister, Tijuana. They were complimenting her on the black suit she was wearing. Tijuana said, "Wow, you look so good. You look like you grew up overnight."

She laughed and said, "I'm not going to grow up. I'm going to be eleven forever."

CHAPTER TEN

Real Men (and Women) Cry

"And if you aren't finished crying, then cry again."

When Asia was born, her mom and dad were the first people she saw. Clifton had always assumed she would be the last person he said good-bye to before he passed on from this earth.

Not to take anything away from his stepson, Isiah— he loves him to death—but Asia was the only Cottom. His brother, David, doesn't have any children, and Asia was his only seed. Her death means the end of the Cottom line. It's hard to heal from something so tragic. But, he'll tell you that he's doing okay. He has found a way.

Asia often had her bags packed on Friday nights to go hang out for the weekend with her friends from school or go to Clifton's friend Bernard and his wife's house, or someplace else. Clifton used to say, "Asia doesn't have time to stand still. She's goin' places." It was almost as if she knew she only had a short while to live, and that's why she did everything so fast.

It was Clifton's childhood friends who stuck with him through everything, and always "had his back." But, his friends felt the loss as well, and also suffered. Clifton's friend, Darryl, worked for the D.C. fire department and had to go through the rubble at Asia's crash site, put out the fires, and pull out dead people and body parts. It took Clifton a whole month to track him down. Darryl couldn't face Clifton. He used to duck him. He used to go out the back door when he saw Clifton coming in the front. Clifton finally caught up with him and sat him down to talk.

Darryl said, "My department didn't know how well I knew Asia and how much I loved her."

Clifton said, "I understand, Darryl. I know."

Dealing with Loss

It is so tough losing a child. Clifton doesn't know when he's going to have a bad day or a good day. Sometimes it gets to him, and sometimes it doesn't. Some days he goes hour by hour, others minute by minute. His mood shifts like the weather. Over the years it has become somewhat easier, and the bad days don't come as often, but they still do come. Everybody means well, but it's hard to understand the pain of losing a child unless you have been there yourself. Clifton believes in the motto "one day at a time."

Clifton was so angry for so long. For a while after her death, he felt like saying to everyone and anyone, "You mess with my family, and I'm gonna come get ya." He knew he couldn't stay in that place of anger because he didn't want his wife and son to see him behind bars or to have to bury him. That's why he shut down. It was safer for him to go to the place of "I don't care."

He held everything in. He wanted to be strong for

Isiah and Michelle, to be the man and take care of them. His pastor, Bishop Ross, asked, "When are you going to cry and release all that pain?" At the time, Clifton didn't even understand what Bishop Ross was asking him to do.

One day, Clifton went into the basement, made sure no one was home, and then he tore stuff off the walls. He screamed and screamed. He got some relief from that, but not much, and then he cried. He cried for four or five days straight. At night, after everyone went to bed, he cried again. On the fourth night he went back to his bedroom, grabbed Michelle, and hugged her and cried and cried with her. At that point he was no longer ashamed to cry in front of her. He still had the same old attitude, but now he was free to release his pain.

Once they cried together he was able to deal with other things in his life as well. For example, one of his friends asked him to meet a friend of his whose son and daughter died in a car accident. The mother saw Clifton smiling and because he seemed to be handling it all so well she thought he was an expert on death and healing. He didn't feel like an expert at all. His daughter died, that's all. And he continues to deal with it and to survive each day.

There are so many things that her death has stolen from him. He can't go to her graduation. He can't chase the boys away. *That's the fun part!* He will miss out on all the days of Asia's life that he would have experienced, if given the chance.

If someone asked him if he was suicidal he would say "Naaaah. That would be the easy way out. So, if anybody says I thought about killing myself, it is not true."

It's Okay to Cry

Clifton wants every man to know it is okay to cry—no matter what pain you are experiencing. And if you aren't finished crying, then cry again. Don't be ashamed. It doesn't mean you are less of a man. Don't cry in private; cry in public. People will respect you more if they see you crying. Believe Clifton when he says that crying was healing in such a way that "holding it all in" could never do.

Every time Clifton talks about it, and every time he helps someone, he feels a little better. He heals a little more. Healing is a life-long process, and he admits he still has a long way to go.

God and Clifton were fighting at the time. God was fighting for Clifton, to get into his heart and heal him. He told Clifton to go to church. Clifton said, "Oh yeah? You think I'm gonna go to church? THERE'S NO WAY!" If Clifton saw a Bible in his house, he would throw it across the room. Bishop Ross and Pastor Jackson talked with him. He tried to listen, but his pain wouldn't allow him to.

In an interview about their experience, Clifton heard Michelle say, "Asia was here on loan." Clifton thought, *Damn, nobody told me that! Why did we get her on loan?* Clifton didn't understand why God would only let them have her for eleven years. He was thinking, *Somebody knows somethin' I don't know? I need to know what is goin' on.*

He was very bitter, but you wouldn't see it, because he hid it well. It took about five or six years before he knew how to change. That's when he knew he needed God in his life again. He knew he needed to start talking to people.

Working on Faith

Clifton is still working on his faith, and will tell you that he wouldn't be here right now if he didn't believe. When you lose a child, it is a whole different world. His faith gives him peace of mind and carries him through.

People always say, "God won't give you something you can't handle." Clifton's response to that was, "Oh yeah? He put it real close to the edge when He took my daughter. If I tilted forward, I would have died. But, God knows what He's doing. I trust Him, even though I still don't get it."

Michelle never forced Clifton to go to church. He would have resented it if she had. She waited for Clifton to go of his own free will. Michelle always said that God loves Clifton just the way he is, and that God wouldn't change Clifton for the world.

Bishop Ross frequently talked to him in order to try to get the old Clifton back, but now with a twist. One of the biggest ways Bishop helped him was by putting him in charge of the youth ministry. Much of his healing came through helping those young men.

Clifton admits that if it weren't for his faith, he would have just gone out and attacked people because it is in his nature. But, he's not going to be able to hold his daughter and hug her ever again, so what's revenge going to do?

CHAPTER ELEVEN

Give Back

"I don't want to keep speculatin' about this and that."

Though his faith was an instrumental part of his healing after losing Asia, he still struggles with many elements of the 9/11 tragedies. There were so many questionable parts to the official story, in New York and Washington, DC, that he's sure it was difficult to piece together the truth of what really happened. But something wasn't right. Clifton was surprised that with all the technology available, that there wasn't more *evidence* of the Pentagon attack released to the public. There were so many cameras pointed at the Pentagon, but there isn't a single picture of the plane. Really? Clifton and Michelle think that those pictures were either stolen or erased, but that we will never know for sure.

One thing is clear: something hit the Pentagon. Clifton doesn't listen to all those conspiracy theories about what really happened.

Clifton said, "This brain is just going to melt down if I discover that what we are being told isn't the truth. I'm a parent whose daughter died. I don't want to keep speculatin' about this and that. It only forces me to deal with it even more than I already do. A movie has been made about 9/11, but I don't want to see it."

Adults Need to Learn Too

It is hard to imagine why the criminals of 9/11 did what they did. Clifton has some ideas about that. "The way I see it, over the years, America became a bully. We go over there and tell them how to vote and how to do things. If a bully keeps pushing, that person's going to come out fightin'. At the school where I work, we deter kids from bullyin' and work with them and make them understand. We are teachin' the kids about the negative effects of bullyin', but we aren't teachin' the adults. Sometimes the adults have a lot more to learn than the kids. We've been botherin' so many countries, and that's why they are coming to retaliate."

One thing led to another, and eventually some man was able to convince some of his people to take Asia's plane and crash it. It's amazing, that someone can talk someone else into doing that.

Clifton wants to say to those men who were involved in the tragic events of 9/11, "Boy, you really got caught by a good motivational speaker if you can be talked into a cause that involves killin' people and children. That's crazy.

"What was in the minds of those criminals? We'll never know. They killed Asia, but what did they get out of it? Tragically, soldiers are returning from the wars overseas with missing limbs, shattered bodies and minds, and some of them aren't coming back at all. It's as if everybody lost somebody in 9/11 or in the wars before and after. *But for what cause?*"

Clifton sees hungry kids every day in his line of work, and it angers him. "There is so much need right here in our own country. If America took care of Americans, focused our energy at home, then we would be okay. Many families don't even know where their next meal is coming from. Some kids are attending school just for a free breakfast and lunch."

Focus on the Positive

In the early stages after Asia's passing, Clifton watched cartoons to keep his mind occupied. But, there were frequent breaking news reports about the war, so even that didn't give him the peace he was seeking. He doesn't watch the news or read the newspapers anymore, just the weather and sports. The rest is just too negative.

For once, he just wants to see all positive news on the front page of one newspaper; reports on something that is going right for a change; no talk about death or countries at war.

After Asia's death, the media often followed them. The Cottoms couldn't stand outside their house without the camera trucks taking pictures. Even to this day, every year, around August/September, the media requests for interviews pour in. The Cottoms took on a press secretary to manage all of it.

Clifton used to grant interviews, but he and Michelle sadly learned that some of the media had their own agenda. He now has some very strong views. "There are some good reporters, but certain individuals wanted to hear what they thought will make a good story, or whatever will promote their cause.

"I tried so hard to be open to the media and the countless requests for interviews. I felt like it was a good way to honor my daughter and to help keep the events of 9/11 alive in the public's memory. I understand that the media has a job to do, but I never became comfortable with how they conducted themselves. I understand that the media has to work within tight margins of time and it is normal for them to take a thirty-minute interview and compact it into five minutes on TV, but this often left me feeling like they were taking out the most important things I wanted to share. My daughter's memory is so important to me. I am sure any of you parents that are reading this would agree with me. It started to feel like: Why did they interview me, if they didn't want to print what I had to say? It's just a waste of my time. If I said anything about the military in Iraq, they'd cut it out. Why wouldn't they let me share my beliefs and faith in God?

"It felt like they were willing to put the words of the most pathetic men on the planet (killers, and molesters) on the air but they were censoring mine. Looking back, the period was so painful that it conjures up negative feelings even as I tell this story now.

"Now I can't tell you for sure why they cut the interviews where they did, but it got so overwhelming for me that I had just back away from the media all together. I needed more time to heal. I had lost my baby girl in the most inhuman and atrocious way possible. I accept what happened to my daughter. I do. And in the process of accepting that, I have found the courage to heal. I finally got a chance to grieve, because I couldn't let myself openly mourn when Michelle and Isiah were still grieving. I guess they say it's the man's role to make sure the wife and son are okay."

One of the "agendas" Clifton refers to centers on interviews that perpetuated the stereotype that all black families don't have both mothers and fathers at home. Asia, Michelle, and Clifton all have the same last name, and they all live together.

"Trust me—I know the female is the strongest species on this earth. My momma raised me, and she did a hell of a job. But, it's the deadbeat dads who always wind up in the news. What about the rest of us? There are a whole lot of us men who are doing all the right things, taking care of our own. Give us some love."

Clifton is an involved father, a provider and protector for his family. He is a good role model and he believes that negative press does a disservice to all dads who are taking care of their loved ones

Giving Back

Despite his pain and frustration, Clifton has found a way to heal. It has been a slow process, but it has happened. One of the biggest parts of his healing was giving back through mentoring kids. There is something about helping others that takes one outside of oneself for a while. Clifton doesn't know what he would have done without those kids.

In the years following Asia's death, Clifton coached the girls' basketball team, and it was great for him. It was a wonderful mentoring opportunity and one of the many steps in his healing process. The girls were eleven, twelve, and thirteen years old. He coached them for about two years before Asia died, and then several years after, so he knew them quite well. Asia wasn't on the team because he never forced his child to do anything she didn't want to do.

He treated those girls on the basketball team as if they were his own. Many of them didn't have a father in their lives, so he played what he called the "two-headed monster." He acted as their dad and their coach. Although the mothers were doing a good job raising them, they still *needed* a father figure. If a young girl sees a positive male role model, she will also want a good husband and a good father for her children; it all ties together.

Some of the mothers would call Clifton and say, "My daughter ain't doin' what she suppose' to be doin'."

Clifton would say, "Put her on the phone." Or, he would go to the house if he had to.

Sometimes these girls would come to him with their problems, mostly about their boyfriends and their family lives. One girl talked to him about an uncle who harshly and loudly criticized her. Clifton recognizes that girls at that age are fragile. If you scream at them, they'll get hurt. So Clifton went over to her house and talked to her uncle and her mother and got everything straightened out.

He helped those girls, but they were also overly protective of him too. They really cared about him. He looks back fondly on that time. *It was a wonderful ride.*

That year the school gave Clifton the "Outstanding Courage Award from Bertie Backus Middle School 2002" because he came back after Asia died and finished up the year coaching the girls.

Learning Through Sports

A couple of years ago, Clifton was coaching the girls' basketball team at a high school. A seventeen-year-old girl was on the team whose first and middle names were Tekia Michelle Shavon. Michelle thinks it's significant that Tekia's middle names are the same as hers and similar to Asia's. It gives them a special bond. Tekia was mad at the world because there was very little love in her family. She only received love from her grandmother, but not from her mother or father. Every day she fought verbally with her family members, and she wound up failing her senior year.

The hardest thing for Tekia to do was to apologize. It was easier for her to fight. She would punch Clifton and cry at the same time. But, he never gave up on her. She finally turned the corner, and he was able to get her to start coming to the church. Michelle and Clifton went to see Tekia graduate from high school, which is a significant accomplishment for her. Recently Tekia was accepted at a community college in upstate New York. Clifton and Michelle are extremely proud of her and all she has accomplished. Clifton is so glad that he was able to play a role in her life.

Clifton won the following awards for his work on the basketball team:

- Spingarn High School Coach of the Year 2012, Girls' Varsity Basketball.

- Clifton Cottom, head coach, Girls' Varsity Basketball. "Thank you for your dedication and love for Spingarn High School Athletics 2013."

CHAPTER TWELVE

Helping Boys Become Men

"I'm not gonna quit on you."

Bishop Ross gave Clifton all kinds of projects to help him with his grieving, but it was the role of youth minister (he preferred to be called youth coach or youth leader) of the young men that helped him the most. When it was first announced he was taking over the young men's group, there was a lot of negative feedback from the church members. They said things like, "He doesn't know what he is doing," or that he wasn't as "holy" as they were because he didn't walk around with a Bible in his hands.

Head of Youth Ministry

Clifton was head of the youth ministry for four or five years. He worked with his good friend, William Spruill. Will taught them the Bible, and Clifton taught them life skills. The boys nicknamed William "Starsky" and Clifton "Hutch." It was a good cop/bad cop kind of thing. They worked really well together.

He had seven young men in the youth group, but only one quit because he thought it was too strenuous. The sixteen to eighteen year olds went to amusement parks and the Hall of Fame, and to Six Flags in Jersey.

Isiah was also part of the group.

One young man named Robert was seventeen years old. His mom and dad were together at the time, but later on they divorced. One day, Robert's mother, Angie, called to tell Clifton that her son was hanging out in a rough neighborhood. So Clifton drove out late at night to where Robert's mother said he would be. Clifton told him to get in his truck so he could take him home. Robert tried to put up a fuss to look tough in front of his friends, and he said he refused to go home to his momma.

Clifton said, "Then where you wanna stay at? Your grandma and grandpa have a small place." So, he got in Clifton's truck, and he drove him home. They had a long talk. From then on, his mother called Clifton during the day or night to come and help with Robert.

One day Clifton went to visit Robert at school, and found him in the hallway, cussing and screaming, and acting like a fool along with his friends. His eyes widened when he saw Clifton coming. Clifton walked up to him and, without saying anything, hit him in the center of his chest, and then kept on walking. Robert didn't get mad or say anything, but afterwards he went to his counselor's office and apologized to her for his rude behavior.

Later that day, his mother called and said she heard what had happened. She was amazed at the influence Clifton was able to have on her son.

Clifton told Robert, "We're gonna survive this war of the streets. We're not gonna let the streets win. I'm not gonna quit on you."

Robert was his most difficult case, but once he "turned the corner" Robert said, "What would I have done without you?" Clifton was the only significant male role model in that young man's life. Clifton went to his graduation, and he is proud of him.

Larry was another one in the group who didn't have a father in his life. So, once again, Clifton took on that role.

One day, Larry was in the hallway, doing his thing, taunting the girls. Clifton watched him for a while and then told him to come over. Larry walked to Clifton with his head hanging down.

Clifton said, "Put your head up, you lover boy. You got a pass this time, but be careful 'cause the girls don't wanna be pulled on. You could get arrested."

Larry wound up having a child with someone. Clifton did a lot of one-on-one talking about his new responsibility as a father, and what that meant. Larry said he understood everything, and he would take care of his own.

Larry said to Clifton, "I don't wanna do what my dad did to me. I won't leave my child."

Another one of the young men in the group named Don had a dad who worked long hours. Don's dad told Clifton he couldn't be there for Don like he wanted to, so he asked him to help out. His dad said to Clifton, "Bust him in the head if he does something wrong."

I'm There for You

Of course, Clifton never had to do that because he preferred to listen and talk with the youth in his group. Don's dad is married to his mother, who was the church administrator and a full-time nurse, so they entrusted Clifton to become a substitute dad whenever it was needed.

Clifton went to Don's class one day to check on him because he wasn't doing his schoolwork, and he was messing around with the other students. Clifton asked, "Wassup?"

Don asked incredulously, "How long you gonna be at this school?"

"How long you need me?" Clifton replied. "You never know when I'm gonna pop up. I'll make sure there isn't nothin' gonna stop you from graduatin'." Don wound up completing high school and ultimately graduated from college. Now he is working and has his own place.

A wonderful mother raised Benjamin, another one of Clifton's young men, in a single-parent home. He was very intelligent, loved to debate any topic, and he is a good man. However, he wouldn't stop using the word "nigger" in his speech.

Clifton warned him to never use that word again, and explained why it is so derogatory. Benjamin listened, and he stopped using that word. He put his energy into his schoolwork, and he is currently studying theology.

Another one of Clifton's youths, Quinton, graduated from college this year. He was expected to do well because he had a dedicated mother and stepfather. As a side note, if someone takes on the role of dad, Clifton believes that he then deserves to be called the real father, not the *step*father.

Another young man in the group, Jeremy, is doing great. He has a daughter he takes care of and works two jobs.

Clifton loved helping those young men, and they still talk and try to get together for reunions, but they are all busy with their families and work, which is exactly what they ought to be doing.

A major step in Clifton's healing process was helping this group of young men. They kept him on his toes, kept him busy, and kept him involved.

The youth ministry also took in other young men from the neighborhood to show them what it was all about. Clifton was doing security work in the church at the time. He had a PlayStation in the back that the young men wanted to play with. Clifton said, "You can do that, but you gotta do security with me and then go to the 8 o'clock church service."

Clifton would also say to them, "If you cross your parents, I'll let you know what's gonna happen to you."

They helped Clifton with the security work by taking turns walking around to make sure all the cars and the buildings were secured. One day, they were roughhousing and running around in the church. Clifton told them, "Because you are showin' off and don't know how to act, you're all gonna sit with your parents in church today." That was the worst (but ultimately the best) thing he could have asked them to do. But, they listened to him and went upstairs and did what they were told. The parents looked at Clifton astonished, and Clifton just smiled proudly back at them.

After the service he asked those kids, "What did the preacher talk about? Did you take any notes?" Then he said, "Don't ever disrespect me, your parents, or the church again."

A Good Role Model

One important thing Clifton learned in youth ministry is that you don't have to have your own kids to be a good male role model and substitute dad to others.

He was extremely honored when his church—and the youth ministry—gave him a plaque that reads: Brother Cottom, A Spiritual Father and a Real Man 2004–2007 Smyrna Youth Ministry. Presented to Clifton Cottom. "You taught us to know our own shortcomings, and still like ourselves, this is what keeps us happy. This lesson has made us stronger and more self-confident."

The syndicated radio announcer, Mr. Tom Joyner, also honored Clifton with a regional award for his work with youth in 2007. He does a morning show called "Real Fathers, Real Men." It is an award that recognizes special men who are providing a good example and making a difference in the lives of others. Michelle thinks it was prophetic that Clifton was listening to Tom Joyner on the radio when Asia died.

Clifton's mission in life is to help young men to "man-up" and take responsibility for their children.

Many men try to blame their upbringing, but Clifton will tell them that that is *no* excuse for them to neglect their children.

Clifton thinks that fathers have to stop being trifling. Clifton often said, "I don't care if you hate the child's mother. You shouldn't make the child suffer. It was okay for you to lie down and have sex with the mother. Now you have a child. To me, a child is a blessing. Take care of your own. It makes me think of you as less of a man if you don't. I will call you out on it."

Clifton told them, "Do me a favor: hug your children for me. That might be the last hug you give them." Clifton's tragedy and the resulting pain have given him a unique perspective on parenting, that's for sure.

There are so many fathers who take the easy way out, and then on the other hand, there are a whole lot of guys taking care of their own and somebody else's, and that is to be respected to the fullest. If one is bitter at the female, it isn't fair to be bitter at the child. There are some people who would be perfect parents and they can't have children, and others shouldn't have children and they do. Everyone must deal with the hand they are given.

The Importance of a Dad

Unfortunately, Clifton's story began without a solid father figure like many of the young men he worked with in youth ministry. His dad used to come around about once a month to take his kids away for the weekend, and for the rest of the time it was Clifton's mother and older brothers who raised him.

When Clifton was in grade eleven or twelve, his dad came around more. His dad said they had to become friends before he became a parent because he wasn't there for him from day one. When Asia was born he became a real grandfather to her and Isiah, and he fully enjoyed their company.

In his latter years, Clifton's dad developed Alzheimer's disease, resulting in him forgetting everyone; even his own sons, but he never forgot Isiah or Asia. Fortunately he passed before Asia did, so he didn't have to witness that tragedy.

Clifton's momma always said, "Make sure your child has a better life than you did."

Clifton needed to get a scholarship to pursue a higher education because his mother didn't have enough money. This is one of many reasons Clifton and Michelle started a scholarship fund in Asia's name, because they both know what a scholarship can do for people.

Asia's passing like she did was unfair and it will hurt for the rest of Clifton's and Michelle's lives, but they are learning to turn something negative into something positive. For Clifton it is all about working with the youth and facilitating the Scholarship Fund. He would rather deal with a child than deal with an adult because the impact one can have on a child's life is truly eternal.

CHAPTER THIRTEEN

Accepting One Another

"There's no I. There's only we"

Friendships are so important. Guys need to do things separately from the women sometimes. Clifton will go with his friends on trips to the Hall of Fame, jazz concerts, and sporting events. They often sit down to talk about their lives. They are real brothers, sharing a tight bond for years. They say things like, "You know what my crazy wife did?"

Clifton's friend Benson has a daughter, Ashley, who was born the same year as Asia. Benson used to coach the boys, and Clifton used to coach the girls in middle school.

One day, when their girls were playing together, he remembers very clearly that the basketball game was over, and Clifton's team had won the first round, and Benson's team won the second. Benson's boys were on the bench, but they were fussing. At first Clifton and Benson didn't know why.

Then they saw Asia and Ashley throwing sunflower seeds at the boys' heads. When Clifton and Benson called the girls over, they laughed and Asia said, "Are those big ol' basketball players crying about sunflower seeds? Yes, we busted them in the head with little sunflower seeds." She and Ashley giggled and ran back to their seats.

Clifton said to Benson, "What are we gonna do with these girls?"

After Asia passed, Clifton asked Benson if he would mind if he spoiled his daughter. Benson said, "There is plenty to go around; sure, I have no problem." Clifton now treats Ashley as if she is his own. When Ashley started college, Benson and Clifton drove her down and helped her to settle in. But Michelle and Clifton couldn't handle going to her graduation because it was still too painful for them to watch this young lady graduate, particularly because Ashley and Asia were supposed to graduate from college at the same time.

Being with Ashley and spoiling her is also part of his healing process. She was one of the recipients of Asia's scholarship fund.

Tough to Admit Weakness

Clifton believes strongly that men should take care of the household, and yet, sometimes, after Asia's death, he still becomes overwhelmed with feelings of loss and grief. He talks to the guys, and he talks to Bishop Ross and Pastor Jackson. Even though he talked with them all the time, he still felt as if he couldn't let them know the times when he was becoming weak. It's so tough as a man to admit any weakness, even if it is justified.

He still hurts. But he's getting closer to peace. Men are expected to be tough. Rugged. They can take care of everything. In Clifton's case, he would die for his children and his family. He has said on more than one occasion, "God why didn't you take me instead of Asia?" But that's not what happened. And this he knows he must accept.

Clifton said, "If Michelle had given me my walking papers in the years after Asia passed, it would have been nobody's fault but my own. I was self-destructing. I was doing things I shouldn't be doing, hanging out by myself, ducking my friends. It's just how I handled the pain. I would say to Michelle or my friends, "I gotta go." And then I would take long drives in my car by myself. Sometimes they knew where I went, sometimes they didn't. Michelle called everybody, trying to locate me."

Finally Michelle and Clifton had a big pow-wow. Michelle told him he had to start releasing his pain. He cried himself to sleep afterwards. But, the next day, the doors were opened a little more. He started feeling again.

In the years following 9/11, Clifton's friends said they would have his back. He said, "I don't want nobody to have my back, I want my daughter." But, they stuck with Clifton, despite what he said, or how he behaved.

Only *WE*

Sometimes, when Clifton tells people his story, they ask, "Why are you not lying on the floor?"

Clifton tells them, "Because my wife and my son keep me off the floor—Michelle and Isiah. There's no *I*. There's only *we*."

Clifton felt guilty towards Michelle because he was the last one to see Asia alive, and the last person to hug and kiss her. He is the one who dropped her off at the airport. He thought he was doing the right thing, that he was being a good father. He talked to the Bishop a lot about all his guilt.

Why do parents divorce when they lose a child? Why leave when you are supposed to be in it for the long haul? When Asia was young, and Michelle and Clifton were arguing, they taunted each other by saying, "When Asia turns eighteen, you go your way, and I'll go mine." She'd be twenty-four years old by now.

They still tease each other with the line, "You still here?"

Whenever Michelle and Clifton argued, they would say what they had to say, then the next morning one of them would ask, "Hey, you want something to eat?" That's how they did it. That's how they survived. Plus, the two trips a year with the guys, and Michelle's outings with her girlfriends helped a lot. As well, for Michelle's 50th birthday he sent her and her seven girlfriends on a cruise; he wanted to show her how much he loved and appreciated her.

Clifton would sit back and listen to Michelle talk about everything—God and the church and needing some "me" time. Clifton said to himself, *if that is what helps her heal, then leave her be.*

Clifton's late mother-in-law, Ann Hargrove, said, "Accept me for who I am, and not for who you want me to be." That's how Clifton is living his life. That's the legacy he wants to leave.

CHAPTER FOURTEEN

A Brother Remembers

"This is who I am."

Asia and Isiah used to have fun with each other. Although he is six years older than her, they often played together, but they also fought like normal brothers and sisters. She made him do things with her he initially didn't want to do … like playing dress up and playing with Barbie dolls. She would even dress him up like a princess, complete with pink clothes and a crown on his head! If he protested she would say, "You gotta do this now or I will call Mommy." But, he will tell you that he secretly enjoyed it every time.

Why? Why?

After Asia's death, Isiah often asked himself and others, *Why did this happen?* He asked God to fix this problem. He asked his parents why this happened to Asia, and his parents told him there is no easy answer for it; it is something they can't do anything about.

Music comes naturally to Isiah, like breathing. He didn't have to study it in school. His mom always said he is a creative person. He has written many other songs, but they are all about having fun and true events. He only writes about actual personal experiences; he doesn't make up any false stories.

Many rap songs focus on guns and drugs and violence. Isiah would rather not talk about such things because that is not the way he was raised. He believes there is no point in saying he killed someone when he never did. He would rather talk about the real world his parents raised him in.

His parents taught him that he shouldn't sell drugs on the streets, or drink and drive, and to treat women with respect. If his sister were alive, he wouldn't want her to deal with men treating her unkindly. Asia was a loving, caring person. And if Asia were alive today, Isiah wouldn't want any man treating her badly. He would want her to receive the same respect that he is giving girls now. If Asia were still here Isiah would want her to go to school and to do whatever she would wish to do. Isiah is very aware of the fact that he gets to do all the things his sister will never be able to experience.

He takes these lessons his parents taught him on "how to live life right," and he uses them every day. And that is what he talks about when he writes music. Some people like it and some people don't. Some people would rather hear all that other negative stuff.

Papercut

He got the nickname "Papercut" in college. A friend of his named Chuck heard him rapping with another kid, and Isiah wound up winning the rap battle. He gave Isiah that name after that. Isiah immediately took a liking to his new nickname. People would say, "You gotta stay away from Papercut he will cut anybody up." And that's why he kept the name.

Isiah, inspired by watching his grandmother cook dinners on Sunday, and from watching the Food Network on TV, decided to go to culinary school. It is another outlet for his creative mind. Right now he is working in the food service department for the Veterans' Hospital. However, he continues to decline the request to make his family a meal! While he enjoys writing his music, he also enjoys his years of cooking. It is his "plan B," because to be safe, one can't just stick to one thing.

When Isiah's friends found out what happened to his sister, they asked him, "Okay, what are you going to do now?"

Isiah said, "I don't know."

His friends would say, "You need to do something about this."

They were suggesting that he should volunteer for the military service to retaliate against the criminals for what happened.

He told them, "That's not going to bring her back."

Everyone wants peace, but we will never have it until we get together as a country and say, "Stop! Stop the fighting."

They knew what Isiah meant, but they were so deeply moved by Asia's death that they felt something needed to be done to prevent further attacks on America.

Isiah's friends were confused and incredibly angry. The majority of them went to Asia's school. They viewed Isiah and Asia as family members.

To add confusion to an already difficult situation, some of Isiah's friends asked him, "What if the plane really didn't hit the Pentagon?" Isiah responded that he really didn't know what to think, and neither did he wish to consider such disturbing thoughts.

After 9/11, the media were constantly bothering the Cottoms. Every time they opened their front door there was an onslaught of cameras and reporters. At one point, Isiah's parents decided to move to a different location so that they could escape the media, and the constant memories of Asia throughout the house. But Isiah didn't want to leave because he was afraid Asia wouldn't be able to find them. He knew she was dead, but what about her spirit?

Isiah, even-tempered, (he had never been spanked) became combative with Michelle and physically tried to push her out of Asia's room when he saw her trying to pack Asia's things. Michelle called Clifton to help her to calm him down.

In order to console Isiah and to get him to comply with the move, Clifton and Michelle took pictures of Asia's room and resurrected it in the new home, precisely like it was in the old one. They put her Barbie Dream House in the window so that she could see it if she were passing by. That was Isiah's idea, so that she would know the Cottoms were inside. Isiah spent time in her relocated room, often playing on her computer or writing music in order to comfort himself. He was always careful not to disturb anything.

Finding Solace

Asia was a popular kid. She also had a lot of cousins and neighbors who were her friends, and they were all torn apart and devastated by her death. Those kids would also go into her room and find peace. For the longest time it was kept exactly as she had left it. His parents still own the original house, and someday Isiah plans to live in it again.

When he was very young, his grandmother initially took him on-and-off to church. But then eventually his mom started going on a regular basis, and then they ended up continuing to go as a family. It took him a while to understand what church was—what it meant for the individual. When he was little he didn't really take it seriously. He used to look at church as boring. He would rather be at home doing something else. But now he will tell you, "What's not to enjoy about it?"

When he was a teenager, sure, he did the things normal teenagers do, like hanging out with his friends and smoking and drinking and partying. Later on that kind of stuff caught up with him, and he heard his inner voice say, *You need to stop it*. Eventually he was no longer content with his lifestyle because it was as if God was telling him it was wrong. When he was hanging out with his friends he would say things like, "Is this all we are doing all day?" Something was missing.

Isiah compares it to having a million dollars. "You can have it all, but it won't make you happy at the end of the day. Money can't buy happiness, and neither does partying, and they both can't bring Asia back."

And that is when he gave up his negative lifestyle. When he did, some of his friends laughed at him. Some of those same friends have children now, and some didn't go to school, and they have to suffer the consequences. And some of them are still doing those same things they were doing all those years ago.

Isiah thanks God he was taken out of that situation. Now he has friends who tell him, "You don't want to end up like me." They say things like, "I have all of this drama with my significant other, I've got children, and it is very hard."

Some of Isiah's friends had children before they were even twenty-one. They are still trying to get their lives together... It's crazy.

There were times when Isiah thought he would never make it. But God always pulled him through. If it weren't for God, he doesn't know where he would be. It's like God has told him, *Now I am going to be your right-hand man.* He still goes to church, and his faith is stronger through all of this. He truly believes that his faith has grown because he gave it all to Him.

Isiah's mom also helped him by telling him that the best thing to do is to pray. So, he prayed a lot with his mom. He would pray about whatever was on his mind at the time, all his thoughts. Although he was incredibly angry with God, and he told Him so, God still comforted him.

Who I Am

He is tired of so many people putting him on the backburner, or making fun of him. Some people would ask him why he acts the way in which he does. He tells them, "This is who I am." People try to change him, but he tells them, "You don't need to do that."

People will stare at him because of the way that he walks. He tells them, "This is just the way I am, I can't help it."

Isiah has learned that God made him this way, and he can't control it, or do anything about it. In some ways, Asia used to help him with all that. She had a strong self-esteem and she was never afraid to do anything. And the best part is that she loved Isiah for *just the way he is.* Now he is happy with himself. He gave it all to God, and he doesn't think about it anymore.

Isiah understands that everybody wants to move forward, and put the pain of losing Asia aside, but there are still a lot of times that he just wants to keep his best friend's (his sister's) memory private. Nobody knew Asia like Isiah did. But now, Isiah doesn't want to keep the story to himself any longer, he wants to let it out because if it were the other way around, and Isiah had perished in that fatal plane crash, Isiah knows Asia would have done everything to tell the story so others would benefit.

He tells his friends all the time he's not big on social media because he doesn't want a gazillion people looking at his personal stuff and then turning it into something else. However, he will use social media strictly for his business, for the music, to let people know where to find it, and for the Scholarship Fund. He hopes his story, told through social media and this book, will motivate others to donate to the Fund.

"Now, I'm kinda glad that we are doing this book because I want people to understand what I am going through. I was trying to make something of myself and whatnot. I have people tellin' me that my music was never goin' to be heard, and I already know right now that they are wrong. I am goin' to be something. This book right here is goin' to affect a lot of people." As crazy as the story of 9/11 sounds, it is not fiction. This really happened.

He is pleased his family has founded the Scholarship Fund in Asia's name because he also wants to help people to get an education, people who otherwise may not be able to.

CHAPTER FIFTEEN

Isiah's Gift

"Sometimes I get mad and show my tears."

Isiah still feels lonely because he misses his sister so much. He misses having her beside him. She was like his right-hand. When she passed, Isiah created music for her. He had to do something because at the time he was very angry and he didn't know what to do with all of his feelings. Creating music was a way for him to deal with his pain.

From Isiah

A Song for Asia

Child Rebel Soldier by Isiah R. Batey (aka Papercut)

Verse 1

We have to stop with this drama

you don't want to bring it to your Momma

why is it we go to war

and our sons and daughters end up on the floor

my life has a purpose in deed

to stay away from the drugs and the weed

most die from fights in Iraq

half of us are never coming back

most of the population is white and black

and we don't need that

we need to stick together

so we can live better

I'm not gonna end up like the Twin Towers

the only way they can clean me up is takin' showers

that's how I feel

and to me that's real

Chorus (2X's)

I'm a child rebel soldier foreigners after me; I told ya

They throwing rocks and boulders and have guns on
their shoulders

Verse 2

We need to clean up this crazy infested land

I don't know how much we can stand

hundreds of soldiers die every year

not because of the liquor here

from the gun shots they get quicker

they're small and they'll hit ya

America help take resources like oil

they does this because they're spoiled

to me that's a bad thing to do

if they do this again we're through

I want war to leave us alone

and our troops to come home

my sister died in 9/11

it wasn't her fault

she just got caught

* * *

To Asia,

A Poem from your brother, Isiah

Alicia Keys sings songs from the heart

America is falling apart

I wonder why people going to war

It remind me that happen before

I fell in basketball got a sore

We need to stop it make me sad

I think Jesus it make glad

I will never forget Asia SiVon Cottom

My mom had to sit her on her bottom

Sometimes I can't watch TV anymore

Because it's an eyesore

I pray for it to be over

Amen

* * *

Heaven Only Knows by: Isiah R. Batey (aka Papercut)

Verse 1:

Heaven only knows like the John Legend record

You wonder how I know, yea I guessed it

Because I've seen my ups and downs

And witnessed my smiles and frowns

I've been through a lot over the years

Sometimes I get mad and show my tears

It comes from life and my brother

And the people who call me a sucker

Excuse me I hope it doesn't stay that way

Because I must get the mic and speak what I say

Like I said the truth is in me

Like my last song the truth is plain to see

Please Bishop preach the Word

While I do the same to the unheard

While this is goin' on I'll pen my message

Then feed the devil the Bible for breakfast

Verse 2:

I went inside to find this verse

When I got finished I knew it would work

Just like Isaiah 40:40 I must relax

Then later I'll feel the raps

Through the process I made a nice song

This is not a party where all the drinks are gone

Because Jesus in heaven will supply all our needs

If we get broke He'll give us the cheese

If my soul did drugs I wouldn't kill him

He would go to rehab like LeCrae and Eminem

All my saints put your hands in the air and wave them
around like you just don't care

Verse 3:

I and LeCrae understand my Daddy's vision;

Because some of ya'll just won't listen

As long as I stay with the faith;

The rest of the drama can wait

Because me and the saints have a new mountain to climb

I want the Holy Father to hear my new rhyme

There are a lot of new rappers spreading the Gospel;

But making it is the new obstacle

I know I can't even praise His name

While they out there sellin' the caine

While that's goin' on He'll help their brain (2x's)

And all ya'll stand up and cheer;

And I want ya'll to do it like it's your last year

This might be it for me

This is the last rap that I might ever speak

CHAPTER SIXTEEN

A Message of Hope

"I believe Asia was on an assignment from God to spread the message of hope."

Asia had a tremendous impact on many people outside of her family. Pastor Herbert Jackson, the Cottom family's Press Secretary and an executive board member of the Asia SiVon Cottom Memorial Scholarship Fund, is honored to serve the family. He is a longtime friend, is one of the many who loved Asia and has learned to look at life differently because of her impact on him.

Smoke and Questions

On the day of 9/11 Pastor Jackson was driving up I-395 toward the Pentagon. He saw an airplane hovering, and was worried that it was flying too low. And then it was gone. He drove a little farther, and then saw a lot of smoke billowing out of the Pentagon. *What in the world is going on?* he thought. Moments later he heard fire trucks and police personnel racing down the four-lane highway, and then they started moving cars off the street.

As Herbert drove on a little farther, the traffic soon came to a standstill. *What is going on?* Then his phone rang; it was his mother. He told her that he was on 395 and on his way to work.

"Get off and get away from the downtown area," she begged him.

When he questioned her, she said, "For once in your life just do it and do not ask me a whole lot of questions." Then his cell phone went dead.

Herbert pulled off the highway and got onto another street, still going towards the downtown area, because it was the only way he could go. People were frantic. He turned the radio on, and the hosts were talking about the planes that hit the Twin Towers and also the one that had gone into the Pentagon. He was dumbfounded, numb, as he listened.

Just the night before, Herbert had spoken to Michelle about Asia leaving to fly to California for her school trip and how excited she was about her adventure. He didn't have a clue that she was on the plane that hit the Pentagon.

Herbert's thoughts immediately went to friends and family who worked in the Pentagon. Were they safe? His niece, Renee, worked there, and he was worried. Later that afternoon she called to say she was safe. He later found out that one person from his church who worked in the Pentagon was very badly wounded, lost an arm and was burned over much of her body. Two of his friends, with whom he bowled, died in the Pentagon. It was a tragic loss of lives.

Asia Was on the Plane

Herbert still had no idea that Asia was on that plane. It was Clifton who called to let him know. A deep anger arose within him and he wondered how he would ever release it. He couldn't talk to anyone about how he felt. There were so many unanswered questions, and when you are close to someone who is a victim, you are also victimized.

In the early stages of the dioceses, several churches came together. Herbert didn't pay much attention to the fact that his children, as well as some of the other children and Asia and Isiah, would sit with his mother in church.

There was an after-school program in the basement of the church that Herbert's mother worked at and where Asia attended the reading program. His mother often talked about the kids in the reading program, but at the time he had no idea that the little girl she was also talking about was Asia. Asia also talked with Michelle about Mrs. Jackson, at the after-school program, but she assumed Asia was talking about one of the teachers; she had no idea she was talking about Herbert's mother.

Another Death

Mrs. Jackson was so shaken by 9/11 but he didn't understand the degree of her anguish because he didn't know how close the two were. When he presided over the memorial service for Asia on September 22nd, his mom was supposed to go with him to the service. However, she called him that morning and said she just couldn't do it. He had no clue as to the depth of their relationship.

During the memorial service, at about noon, one of the ushers from the church called Herbert down from the pulpit to say that his mother was being rushed to the hospital and he needed to attend to her immediately.

He left the memorial service still fully clothed in his clergy attire. When he arrived, he saw his brothers and sisters standing in front of the hospital. "What is going on? Where's Mom?" he asked.

Karen, his sister, appeared shaken when she said, "I was talking with Mom on the phone when all of a sudden she stopped speaking. I tried to call her back, but the phone was busy. So, I called the paramedics."

They all hugged each other and then went into the hospital. After they had waited anxiously for the doctor for quite some time, he finally approached them and said their mom had passed.

"That's impossible," Herbert said.

The doctor gave him a questioning look.

"My mother wouldn't go someplace without telling me she was going." He felt the panic beginning to rise within him.

The doctor turned to the nurse and instructed her to get the sedation kit. Karen grabbed Herbert by the arm and said, "No, no I have him."

After Herbert gained his wits about him, he walked into his mother's room and when he came out, he had the funeral home on one phone, and had their pastor

Reverend Walls on the other. Right then, Herbert completed the funeral arrangements. Days later, he conducted the eulogy, and preached his mother's sermon. However, the stress was compounding, but he didn't realize it at the time.

For his mother to pass on the 22nd and Asia on the 11th of September was very hard on him. His mother wasn't sick and she was only sixty-two-years old. They were very close. To this day, the doctors cannot come up with a conclusive cause of death. His mom was a very active part of their church, and her death impacted their congregation in a very powerful way. He also felt he should minister to all the families who were torn and hurt by 9/11 and his mother's death. It was a lot to deal with.

Michelle and Herbert soon learned that Herbert's mother was the same Mrs. Jackson Asia always referred to. This realization occurred during his mother's funeral service and brought their families closer together.

Compassion Through Experience

A pastor friend of Herbert's called him about six months after his mother died. He was glad for the call because he needed to talk with someone.

"I'm having one of those bad days," Herbert said.

"What's going on?" he asked.

"I'm just having a really bad time. I'm thinking about and missing my mom so much."

"You aren't over that yet? You need to get over that."

Herbert was indignant. *Get over it? You never get over losing someone like that.*

"Call me back when *your* mother passes," he said. Conversation over.

About eighteen months later Herbert saw the same pastor standing in the corridor at a conference they were attending. Herbert thought, "I really don't feel like dealing with this today."

The pastor walked up to Herbert with a strange look on his face, and said, "Herb, can we talk?"

"...Sure."

The pastor said that his mother had passed.

Herbert said, "We can talk now."

The pastor hung his head. "What I said to you I will never say again to anybody."

Herbert thought, *at times pastors don't know when to be quiet.* Sometimes they need to know when to stop talking and when to listen.

Too Much Stress

Herbert doesn't talk about this very much, but in December of 2002, he became deathly ill as a result of the stress being too much—so much so that the doctors told his family they should start planning funeral arrangements.

He was paralyzed. He became blind. He lost so much weight that he dropped to 118 pounds. It was just an awful time. From 2002 to 2003 his condition continued in that way, and he was finally diagnosed with a form of anemia. The stress and the depression simply caused his body to shut down.

It was a hard two years. Herbert was off work for eight months, but he didn't lose any checks. His children remained in private school. The church kept going. God was surely faithful.

While he was in the hospital, Michelle and Clifton came to visit, and he remembered so vividly Michelle standing there in the doorway. She didn't say a word, but the look on her face said, "You can't do this. You can't die on us."

Herbert was finally released from the hospital after a long stay. Two days later his father passed. His family told him he would not be presiding over the funeral, which was incredibly hard on him. Prior to his father passing, his great aunt died and then his pastor died. *It just didn't end.*

When Herbert finally went back to pastoring, he became very skeptical about riding on a plane, which is impossible for him because he needed to fly for his work all the time. So, with prayer and determination, he forced himself to the place where he had to determine that *he must live again*. And that was true for all those who loved Asia.

Michelle says, "Clifton and I supported Herbert through that difficult time, and we became very close. Herbert believes Asia put everyone together to become one family. To this day, if he has to tell someone about something he is going through other than his wife, he first calls his sister, Karen, and then me."

Requests for Interviews

Every year, during the 9/11 time frame, the press comes to the Cottoms with requests for interviews starting about the last week in August. The executive board has opted not to do a lot of interviews. Herbert writes the press releases because he knows the family's heart. He makes sure that what the press wants lines up with the Fund's focus.

Herbert wants to make sure the media recognizes the sensitive nature of what a family is going through in the loss of a child. His job is to make sure the press recognizes that Michelle and Clifton have lost a daughter, without sensationalizing the events. He wants to make sure that their family is not "put on display."

Herbert says that Asia's message is a message of hope. He believes Asia was on an assignment from God to spread this message.

CHAPTER SEVENTEEN

The Importance of Sharing and the Right Environment

"No one really understood all the ties."

Herbert notes that it is important that Asia's story is told as it relates to what they experienced and what they continue to experience on a daily basis. It is profound to realize what an impact Asia, from an early age, had on so many people. She was truly one of a kind.

Herbert has two children who were very close to Asia, a son two years younger and a daughter three years older. But they were all together, for the most part, through their family ties, and their churches still come together to do many things. Herbert's children talk to him about their feelings about losing Asia. They also tell others that they were friends with one of the victims of 9/11. The impact of this tragedy goes above and beyond the Cottom family; it affects so many people in so many different ways.

When the media displays pictures of the horror of that day, it doesn't work really well for all those affected by 9/11. Herbert tries to manage the annual onslaught of the media by telling everyone what is about to come out so that they can prepare people. They have also learned to manage what the children would see or hear in the papers and radio and TV, and have taught them how to deal with the media.

Herbert said, "We had to really understand the children's feelings about it. "My son told a story about sitting in class one day when they were talking about 9/11. He asked to be excused. The teacher asked him why, and he had to tell her that his god-sister was one of the victims. It made the teacher realize that maybe she should do this a different way. No one really understood all the ties there were to all the victims of 9/11."

Asia's Impact

Herbert noted that Asia had an impact on people. She was a bubbly little girl. She loved life. She was respectful before her time. She had no problems asking you whatever her topic was for the day, and she waited patiently for you to answer. One day as he went to a dollar store to buy some gum, Asia was there and she called out, "Hi, Uncle Herbert!" (Asia always called him that because that's what his niece called him. As a result, all the other kids in the church started calling him that as well.) He turned around and saw her smiling face and asked her if she wanted a piece of gum. He gave the package to her. She opened it, took a stick of gum out, and handed it to him, and then she put his gum in her purse and said thanks. That's the type of bubbly person Asia was, and he smiled knowing that he had just given her his packet of gum.

Asia always wanted to give everyone a hug before she left to go anywhere. She would always make certain to say good-bye. Herbert notes that everyone feels robbed by not seeing her grow up. What a wonderful young woman she would have become.

It was quite some time later that Herbert was told that Asia's body had been recovered and that it was the impact of the crash, not the fire, that killed her. Her body was so intact that there would have been an open casket funeral, had they recovered and identified the body earlier. It was as if she was asleep when the plane crashed. He believes this meant that God didn't allow her to suffer.

Herbert had agreed to do Asia's burial service until he found out she was going to be buried in the same cemetery as his mother. He had no idea until the day before the burial. When he heard that he said, "Stop! That is where my mother is buried. I can't do it!" It was still much too painful, and he knew Michelle and Clifton would understand.

Talking and Healing

This is a story that needs to be told, but people also need to be ministered to. There is so much healing that needs to be done. When Herbert talks about Asia, he also talks about his mother, and the impact Asia had on her. He talks about Asia hugging him, and he talks about the influence she's had on his children. All of this brings him into deeper healing.

"As Michelle tells the story, I can see her ministering to so many other women. And if she tells her story, Clifton has to tell his story," said Herbert.

Herbert notes that many men don't want to talk to women, or even to him, about their pain. But, they will talk to someone like Clifton, who is perhaps less polished. People will tell Herbert, "I don't know all those fancy words you use, I don't know how you do that." These people feel more comfortable with Clifton.

Minister to Others

Herbert has reached a place in his life where he can proclaim, "You can live again, even after such a tragedy." And even if another's tragedy isn't the same as Clifton's and Michelle's, everyone needs to be ministered to. Asia's story of hope needs to reach the masses. Up until now it has been a story kept mainly in the churches. But now it must go beyond. Asia's story needs to become an evangelism tool to bring healing to others.

"Michelle is not one of those typical church girls," Herbert said. "And Clifton is not a typical church guy, either. People see that you are dealing with a real family that has experienced a real traumatic tragedy, but they overcame it, and they are living through it. And as a result of them living through it, the life of the child continues. We don't even speak of Asia in the past tense. She is still here. We talk about her all the time.

"The first thing that needs to happen in order to heal is that you need to recognize that you *need* healing.

This is more difficult than it sounds. Many people bury their pain because they don't want to deal with it.

"Even though it hurts, and even though I may not understand it, because I trust God, I can get through this. I trust God to carry me through, to make it all right, to show me what it is that I need to learn. I believe that for everything that happens, there is something to be learned. I think that the learning sometimes means that someone else will benefit from it."

The Right Environment

Herbert says that the second step in the healing process is that a person needs to find the right environment. "This includes the people around you, the place itself, and to have enough courage to put yourself in a place that you are able to release. To be with the right people means to be with people who won't judge you or with people who understand that crying is healing. If I had been in a place where I had received healing right away, I don't think I would have become sick.

"Know that it is okay to release. Find some way to talk about the fact that you need to cry and be okay with it. Don't have any regrets about mourning. Don't blame yourself. Let it come out. If you're not done crying, cry again. Tears are healing.

"God does things in His own way, and sometimes we don't understand it. Our hope for this book is that it will be an instrument of healing for the nation."

CHAPTER EIGHTEEN

The Effects of 9/11

Keeping Asia's Memory Alive

It is now thirteen years later, but, through the Asia SiVon Cottom Memorial Scholarship Fund, Asia still lives on. Many graduates have benefitted from the scholarship fund. It is sobering to think that Asia would have been a college graduate by now. Helping the scholarship fund to function well is part of going on. Asia's legacy also lives on as a result of the people the fund is able to help.

"Sometimes you hear about these things happening and then three or four years down the road, the tragedy and the people involved are forgotten," said Herbert. "I follow the commitment the Cottoms have that we keep Asia's memory alive through the scholarship fund. It is through the efforts of Asia's parents and their many friends that others have an opportunity to go to college."

Herbert is encouraged with the fund's direction and purpose. He wants to work with the media to tell the true story of what they are doing. The truth is that Clifton and Michelle are not strung out over the loss of their daughter, nor do they take drugs and alcohol. The true story is they are parents who took this tragic event and they are standing and building upon it—through all of their hurt—and they do this every day.

"People who love others, as the Cottoms do, do not perpetuate hate," said Herbert. "We become at odds with one another in the world, which is the opposite of what we believe."

"Clifton and Michelle's message is one of hope. Sure, sometimes they get down and they wonder, 'Why me? ' But they don't stay there. They get back up, and they move on. If Clifton sees a girl in distress, he goes out to help her. The type of message that he gives with his life is that we are each other's keepers.

"It would be easier to just be nasty souls. But that is not who they are. Despite their pain, and grief, and tremendous loss, you see them wanting to raise money so that other people will benefit through the fund."

Herbert's son is one of the scholars of the fund. When he applied for the scholarship, he was asked to write an essay on how 9/11 affected him on the day it happened and how it still influences him today. As a twenty-two-year-old, he can write about it.

The Effects and Aftermath of September 11th on Today's Society

When I look back on the terrifying event that took place on September 11, 2001, words cannot express the grief and horror that the United States of America endured. During this time, many individuals lost their lives, and loved ones were taken from them in the blink of an eye; but through this tragedy, our country grew in strength and wisdom. Our ancestors stood on the statement, "In God we Trust." Through all of the devastating events that took place on that day I believe not only did our country grow in strength and wisdom, but also with understanding that in all things, our trust in God is beneficial in our lives. September 11th had a great impact on my life. Even though I was young, the pain and devastation affected my life just as it did many Americans around the country.

Eleven years ago on Tuesday, September 11, 2001, my life was impacted and changed forever. I was a fourth grade student at the Nannie Helen Burroughs Elementary School in Washington, DC. As my teacher, Ms. Davis, was passing around the math test we were scheduled to take that morning, the 6th grade teacher from across the hall came running into our classroom instructing Ms. Davis to turn on her television immediately. As my teacher turned on her television, my class began to see the devastating events that were taking place just a few miles away from our school, and everyone became terrified.

During that time I was not fully aware as to what actually caused this tragedy and why someone would display such obnoxious behavior. As the buildings that were hit were named on the news that morning, I recognized two of the buildings being shown. One was the Pentagon, and the other was the World Trade Center. I knew the Pentagon because my cousin worked there and, as a result, I became worried and concerned for her life. Thankfully, later on that day we discovered that she was able to get out of the Pentagon safely.

As the day progressed and as families were searching all over to find loved ones who were trapped in the rubble from the planes crashing into the buildings, my family was also in search for two individuals who were close to our hearts. That night my father, Pastor Herbert H. Jackson, Jr. of The Life-Changing Church called for a prayer service to pray for those families who had lost loved ones in the horrible tragedy that took place that morning. During the prayer service he informed the church that one of our very own, Mrs. Luticia Hook, who worked on the side of the Pentagon where the crash occurred, was rescued and recuperating at the Washington Hospital Center. He then announced that my friend, Asia Cottom, whom I had recently befriended at Randall Memorial Church, was on the plane that hit the Pentagon. When I heard this disturbing news, I was filled with much grief and my heart went out to her family and those who were closest to her. I met Asia through my grandmother, Mary Louise Jackson, and whenever we would fellowship with Randall Memorial, Asia and I would sit with my grandmother. She and Asia had a very close relationship and, sadly, my grandmother passed away on September 22, 2001. Even though Asia is gone now, she still holds a special place in my heart, and I will always cherish her as my friend.

In conclusion, through all of this I have been made the better. Even though 9/11 didn't affect me physically, it certainly affected me emotionally. For months America was in awe of the attack that was placed on our country. The terrorists thought that this attack would defeat our country and make us weak, but in reality this tragedy helped our country grow to be a better people. As a result, I am determined to pursue my dreams of continuing my education and becoming equipped with the tools and resources necessary to impact our great country and the world for all people.

CHAPTER NINETEEN

Comfort My People

"There were no words I could say to comfort them or myself."

Asia came to Bishop Earl Ross's door three times to say good-bye before her trip on the Sunday prior to her passing. Every time she came, someone was in his office. Not one to break in, she kept poking her head in the door to check if he was available. She was much too polite to interrupt. Unfortunately, she was never able to say good-bye to him. That was the last time he saw her.

Remembering 9/11

Bishop Ross remembers that day of 9/11 so clearly. It was early in the morning when he heard about the planes hitting the Twin Towers on the television. It was Clifton who called him. "Bishop, I think my daughter ... I think my daughter was on that plane."

Bishop's heart sank. *I thought it wasn't real. It just couldn't be.* He jumped in his car and drove to their house where people were already gathering. But once inside, there were no words he could say that could offer comfort – including to himself. He walked aimlessly from the dining room to the living room to the kitchen. He kept looking for someone to appear in the door and say *Asia missed the flight* or that she got on the wrong plane.

Asia Angel

Asia was one of the sweet little angels in Bishop's church. She was in everybody's heart. Asia was everybody's child—from the youngest to the oldest. She was what others would call an ideal child. She was very courteous in how she spoke with people and interacted with those around her. If the older people were talking, she would never break in or cut across; she would always go around them. She exuded respect.

Bishop remembers that Asia had a smile that could light up the world. She still smiles at him in dozens of pictures around his office. Asia always knew she had a special place in his heart.

Every Sunday, around 10:30 a.m., Asia would look in and see if anyone was in Bishop Ross's office. Then she would go straight to his desk, sit in his chair, open the drawer, and get some chewing gum from it like he said she could. If there wasn't any, Asia would say, "Hey, where's the chewing gum?" Bishop found himself making sure that he stopped somewhere and bought some gum to always have in the desk. Asia had that kind of effect on people. He no longer keeps gum in his desk drawer.

No Fear

Even though her ordeal must have been terrifying, Bishop felt that she didn't have any fear in those last moments, though no one will ever know for certain. Knowing Asia and her spirit, Bishop said that she may have even been sharing her faith to other people on the plane. She may even have been in her seat asleep. As Bishop noted, "Even the mortician who prepared her body said, 'She was such a pretty little girl, and she just had one little smudge of dirt on her face.'"

The teacher who accompanied Asia was an older, Christian, ex-military woman. Bishop said that he believes that her instincts would have kicked in, and she would have made sure nothing happened to Asia.

"I believe the Lord would have taken her without any pain," said Bishop. "My belief lines up with Scripture in Matthew 8:23–26 when Jesus was asleep in the boat with his disciples, and a furious storm arose. His disciples feared for their lives while Jesus slept soundly. When they awakened Jesus, He said to them, 'Have no fear.' Powerful words. Jesus doesn't want his children to be afraid. "

Bishop Ross dedicated Asia when she was three months old, baptized her at six years old, and eulogized her at eleven. The memorial service for Asia was held in his church, New Smyrna Missionary Baptist Church. The response and support for Asia was unprecedented and overwhelming.

For Bishop Ross, the grieving has diminished, but there is always something happening in society that brings Asia back fresh in his mind. "It is one thing to read about it from far away and be removed from the consequences of the tragedy, but when you come close to the heartbreak of it, it's truly unreal."

Every September 11th Bishop Ross notes that it is like September 11, 2001, especially if you are in Washington, DC. The media coverage usually starts the first of September and then goes all the way through. As someone close to the pain of the event, this can be difficult to deal with. To this day, he cannot fully come to grips with this senseless act. Asia was an innocent in this unprecedented act of evil. Even with his immense faith in God, he still has unanswered questions. He constantly asks the Lord, *Why?* We may never know.

Living God's Purpose

Bishop noted that Asia accomplished God's will in her short life. About Asia he often says, "For this purpose you came into this world at this time." Asia's life affected so many people in countless positive ways. So, for this cause, came Asia at this particular time. "She was not ours to keep."

Bishop has a big heart and he grieves over the fact that Clifton's "bloodline" ended with Asia. She was her father's only child and Clifton's father's only grandchild. Her father's brother (David) never married nor had any children. There are no more Cottoms. His seed ends with him.

Knowing Clifton's demeanor, Bishop realized that he was a ticking time bomb in the earlier years after the tragedy. He initially kept all the pain and grief bottled up inside, slowly eating away at his soul. But he is grateful that God helped Clifton to heal through his work he does with other kids. Bishop's challenge was to help Clifton deal with the heartbreak of losing his daughter while continuing to help other children fulfill their dreams. At first, this was a heartbreaking experience for the both of them, but by working together they have both reached a "good place."

Her Last Thoughts

Sometimes Bishop has wondered what Asia was thinking during those last moments. He has surmised that her favorite scriptures might have filtered through her mind as the chaos in the plane began. Asia's Bible, which was presented to her on March 18, 2001, half a year before she died, is highlighted with her favorite texts. A review of the highlighted text seems to indicate that she knew what was pending.

Bishop said, "Most of the time Asia was leading the way and rushing off to one of her many church activities. She served in several ministries in church, such as ushering, the choir(s), and our dance ministry. She wasn't your typical child in Sunday school either. Asia was energetic and serious about her faith in God. Here are some of the Bible passages she kept on her computer desk and the New King James Version Bible passages she had highlighted. It is as if she is speaking to us through texts such as Micah 6:8, Ephesians 3:10 and 4:11-13, Acts 9:36–42, Daniel 5:13–17, and Revelation 21:8."

Two weeks prior to 9/11, Asia wanted to see her aunt, and she also wanted to go see the people she knew in the reading program. When you look at it in hindsight, it was almost as if she was saying good-bye to people.

How does one move on after such a senseless tragedy? Bishop Ross said, "That is something you don't learn in books." Bishop has been a pastor for over thirty-five years and he was like a grandfather to Asia. In fact, he and Michelle's father were friends and that's another reason he is still learning how to go on but he stands firm on his statement that "Time and God have a way of bringing us to a place of acceptance, and acceptance is the beginning of healing."

What was Asia thinking during those last moments? Bishop Ross always asks families who have lost someone, "What were the last things she/he said or did in the days prior to passing?" From that he gets some direction as to what to say in the eulogy. He asks, "What message was the person trying to convey to us?"

Asia told her parents, "Someday my name will be all over the Internet." She was right! Her story, and the stories of those who knew and loved her, is being told.

CHAPTER TWENTY

Healing Through Writing

A Letter From Bishop Ross

"The book of Ecclesiastes states, 'To everything there is a season, a time for every purpose under heaven: A time to be born, and a time to die.' God's got a reason for not letting this tragedy die. He's up to something. "

One of the best ways to begin a journey of healing is to write a letter to the one who has been lost. Bishop Ross did just that in the following letter.

Given Once, For All - Jude 3

A Letter to Asia

As I sit and think about the many things that I could say about you, there is but one thing that lingers in my mind, and that's the thinking of our Lord's brother Jude, "Given Once, For All."

For this is a summons that only those who are spiritually in shape can answer. It is a summons to only those who will emerge in battle when the truth of God is attacked. It is a summons to come when the dangers are real and one's life is on the line. Yet you are compelled to challenge false teachings and to contend for the faith at the cost of your life for you believed, and I believe that you believed, that 9/11 did not catch you off guard. Its challenge was great, but the God who sent you was even greater. And you were given "Once for All."

I think often of how many times you looked into my office trying to tell me you were leaving on your trip. But now I know why you were never able to do it. For I, in ignorance, may have prayed something that may have interfered with the divine plan of God.

I sit so often and I think about you and what it must have been like at the end. I think about you every time I am on an airplane and it's about to make its landing. I think about the sounds and the way it feels as the plane falls through the air, the bumping, and the shaking as it defies the laws of gravity. Yet I feel somewhat assured of my safe landing. In fact, I am so sure of my safe landing until my concerns are directed to how fast I can get my bags from the overhead compartment and be the first to get off the plane. But still, I think about you in those last moments as *that* plane fell from the sky and the bumping and the shaking and the sounds of fear and death that filled the air. And I wonder if it was then that they could, if only for a moment, see the Christ in you as their hope, "Given Once, For All."

I've got to close now. But there is one thing I must say before closing ... the one thing that I forever keep on my mind. And that was the statement that the FBI agent made to me. I don't remember all of what was said to cause him to say what he said, but he said to me, with a strange look on his face, that there was enough of your remains to have had a viewing and a service with an open coffin. I am sure that smile was still there for I believe that you saw His face. In the midst of all the turmoil, in spite of all the death and surrounded by all the destruction, you saw His face and before death could claim your body, your spirit was in the presence of the Lord.

Good night, Asia. I'll see you in the morning.

CHAPTER TWENTY-ONE

Finding Closure

"No Laughing Matter."

The Cottoms stress the importance of having a memorial service. Why? Because this is where healing begins for many people. What you are about to read brought back so many good memories of Asia. While you may not follow the same faith as Clifton and Michelle, nevertheless, a service such as this helps to bring closure, which leads to acceptance, and finally to healing.

Of that time, Michelle says, "We were overwhelmed by the love and support of our friends, family, and colleagues through this very difficult time, and are thankful for the thoughtful memories, songs, prayers, poems, and tributes that were presented on this day." Pastor Jackson was the worship leader, and Bishop Earl Ross gave the eulogy *"No Laughing Matter."*

The following is an excerpt of the eulogy as it was presented on September 22, 2001.

Pastor Herbert Jackson: For this is an occasion that in the midst of all sorrow we will search for a reason to give glory. We have come to celebrate a life, not a partial life, but a whole life that was given to God.

Bishop Ross: What a mighty God we serve. He is wonderful today. It's a celebration. It's a celebration of life. When you know where you are going, you can celebrate. And we know where Asia is.

Everybody loved Asia. She made friends fast with both the young and the old. She was the love of her family. As long as I can remember, every Sunday morning you could find Asia sitting in my chair. I laughingly said to the parents when it was sanctioned that she was on board, I said, "She is probably sitting in heaven, just like she used to come and sit in my office chair."

I remember her that last Sunday before she passed. I had a number of visitors in my office that day. She had this way, that if others were in my office she would look to see if I was going to give her permission, or give her the eye, to come on in. But, this Sunday morning she just stuck her head in the door and waved at me and said, "Pastor, I am going on a trip, and I will see you when I get back." Little did I know that she couldn't come back to me; but if I live right, *I* can go see *her*.

Asia always attended the midweek service. On that Wednesday before she passed, she got up from where she usually sat in the back row. And I noticed, as she made her way around the room and spoke to her mother, that all of a sudden Asia had begun to lose her baby fat. And right before my eyes, I saw another one of my babies being transformed into womanhood. It struck me that she has been right before me all these years and, all of a sudden, and it was just a matter of days that she looked like she had grown up.

And as I thought about that, I wondered why I didn't see her anymore, and then it dawned on me that it was because she was always either in the choir behind me singing or in the missionary service or ushering. She was never a bench member. She was a working member.

She had a way and a smile that would light up any room, always causing you to love her. And when a personality like that is taken from us, that is no laughing matter.

Asia was in every youth choir and every youth ministry. She was in our dance ministry. She was one of our junior missionaries. You name it, and she was a part of it. And yet, at age eleven she was killed.

Asia died on this side. But she is blooming on the other side. She is becoming a beautiful flower in the garden of God. And we praise God for the life of Asia.

CHAPTER TWENTY-TWO

Letters and Tributes

In the aftermath of 9/11, the Cottoms received many letters of condolences. You will see from these letters that Asia's death didn't just affect her family and friends and all those who knew her, but it affected a nation.

A Sample of Letters received by the Cottom family

Comfort in prayer and condolences

William Jefferson Clinton

September 18, 2001
Clifton and Michelle Cottom
C/O Pearl Barber
5303 4th Street, NW
Washington, DC 20011

Dear Clifton and Michelle,

I was saddened by Asia's untimely death and wanted you to know I'm thinking about you and your family.

This senseless tragedy has disrupted all of our lives but cannot diminish your own personal loss.

Though we can only imagine the grief you are experiencing, Hilary and I hope the support of loved ones, along with good memories of Asia's meaningful life, will give you some solace in this difficult time.

You will be in our prayers.

Sincerely,

Bill Clinton

* * *

Children First

Paul L. Vance

Superintendent

District of Columbia Public Schools

September 18, 2001
Ms. Michelle Cottom and family
5057 Sargent Road, N.E.
Washington, DC 20017

Dear Ms. Cottom:

While no amount of passing time will provide relief from the pain of your loss, I want you to know that you and your family will continue to be in my thoughts and prayers. The teacher in me wants so desperately to explain this somehow—to put it into perspective and make it easier to understand, but I cannot. There are no answers to explain why.

I pray that you will find comfort in prayers and

condolences of family and friends, but also in knowing that Asia lives on in memories of those who were privileged to share her life. Just as she brought joy into your world, she brought joy and inspiration to the world of so many others—the friends she played with and looked out for and the teachers who watched her grow. It is clear that she truly enjoyed life and believed in its promise.

Every day, we are faced with decisions about how to spend out talents and our time. Every day, we decide if we will do good unto others, practice the Golden Rule, and give of ourselves in an unselfish way. If we, as human beings, will choose to do good and to do things that promote the well-being of others, then good will overcome evil and no life lived will ever be in vain. Please share my sentiments with your entire family and call upon your DCPS family should you need us. We are here for you and will keep you in our prayers.

Sincerely,

Paul L. Vance

Superintendent

A Sampling of Letters from Children

Dear Mr. and Mrs. Cottom,

I am very sorry that had to happen. When Miss. D. Johnson told me, I was sad and did not know her. My heart was pounding when I heard that so many people died. I know Asia had many friends and was a nice girl and that her life was taken very early, but she is in a better place and one day you all will meet up with each other. I will always keep her in my heart and other people will too. I hope you feel better.

From Doneher Hale

* * *

Dear Mr. and Mrs. Cottom,

I know about 9/11 but just remember ...

That our flag is still there and we will never forget Asia or anybody else and we will catch the man with the long beard.

Love, Christen Gillis

* * *

Dear Mr. and Mrs. Cottom,

I would tell you that your little girl seems nice. And what happened to her is not.

I know you love her very much. Although she is gone to people, she is not to you because she is still in your heart.

Sincerely,

Justine

* * *

Dear Mr. and Mrs. Cottom,

Ms. D. told us about what happened to Asia, and I'm very sorry such a thing had to happen. No one should have had to go through the things you went through. You should cherish all of the good times you all had and know you made her life good. Try to remember her smiling face, the times she made you laugh and cry. She is probably watching over you now. The nation is doing everything it can so no one will go through this again.

Sincerely,

Nailah Robinson

* * *

To the family of Asia, Asia was a classmate I will never forget. She did not start any trouble or confusion. Asia wanted to be a singer, but she could not live up to it because she passed away. I'm sorry she had to die in such a foolish way.

Sincerely, Darryl

* * *

Her spirit will always watch over her family and her loved ones! Rest in peace. Asia Cottom, you are an angel now.

Sincerely Tovon

* * *

Into the hands of God Asia Cottom shall be. Blessed by her family and every one that knew her very well. And the birds of heaven shall keep you safe! Rest in Peace.

Your friend, David

* * *

Dear Cottom Family,

I'm sorry about what happened to Asia. But Asia has gone to heaven where she has no problems. She was a nice person.

Sincerely, Walter Douglas. We miss you.

Some of the Visitors' Comments taken from www.september11victims.com

This site is dedicated to the victims of September 11, 2001 tragedy.

Victim of Flight #77 Asia Cottom, 11, Washington, DC

David Kaiser: When I heard about Asia Cottom's death, I felt horrible. How could people harm such an innocent, young child? The girl was only eleven, yet was taken away from this world in such a horrible way. Worst, she didn't have the love and support of her family when she died. God bless Asia Cottom and the Cottom family. I keep her and all other children on the planes in my prayers.

Angie: To the parents of this beautiful angel. I can't imagine what you have endured. My heart breaks for you over and over again. I want you all to know that you are in my prayers every day. The Lord will be your strength when you all need it. He will take care of your every need if you just ask. God bless you all and stay strong.

Chad: May God Bless You! You are an angel from heaven, looking down from us. Although we do not know why, we will know someday. I am so sorry, sweetie; today I turn 19, and it just doesn't seem right. What did I do to live eight more years than you? I never met you, but you are a child, we were both 11, we forever share a common bond. May you watch over your family and give them strength to move on. You are truly a blessing! My deepest regrets, Asia.

Kam Nielson: I don't know what to say. Such a young life taken away, my prayers go out to the family.

Jesseca: When I heard that children were on that airplane, my heart sank. I know her mother misses her baby every day. I saw her mom on television, and she said Asia loved the Lord with all her heart. She was not alone on that tragic day for the Lord was with her and may He bless her family and be with them always.

* * *

Michelle and Clifton's response to the outpouring of love: Sweet Asia is indeed safe in her eternal home, forever at peace, basking in the perfect joy and beauty of the everlasting light. Though we still ache to hold her in our arms, we find comfort in the fact that she is in the arms of her Savior.

We want to say thank you to the many people who grieved with us in our time of sorrow and still pray for us and support us when our hearts break again with the loss of our precious girl. Every word, every letter, every prayer, every thought, every hug, and every song lifted us up and continues to sustain us through the difficult times. God bless you.

CHAPTER TWENTY-THREE

A Private Tour of the Pentagon

A Mother's Reflection

Several of our friends and family and the executive board of the ASC Memorial Scholarship Fund accompanied Cottom, Isiah, and me to the Pentagon Memorial on June 4, 2011. Due to the sensitive nature of all the events of 9/11 I was never mentally ready to attend the memorial services held for the victims of Flight #77 that would include specific Pentagon dedications. Unless it was an event specific to Asia or the three DCPS students, it was simply too much for me personally to bear. Cottom and I differed in this respect because he always wanted to attend anything that was associated with Asia's name. Perhaps it was selfish of me, but I never considered how Cottom and Isiah felt regarding these public displays and tributes, but I wanted no part of any of it.

Asia wasn't a patriot who gave her life for her country. She was an innocent little girl who got caught up being in the wrong place at the wrong time. She was just living her life. Nevertheless, I reluctantly agreed to reach out to the folks at the Pentagon to arrange a private tour for the ASC board and some close family and friends. They were so excited to provide us with a special tour, in part because we had declined all previous invitations to attend any Pentagon functions and also because they were generally just kind and gentle people ready to assist us and help add closure to our pain in any way possible. Not only did they escort us throughout the external memorial, but they also gave us a guided tour of the chapel inside the Pentagon, and we saw where the plane had crashed into the wall. It had been completely rebuilt within a year.

One single brick from the original part of the damaged building is inscribed "September 11, 2001." There is a dedication wall, a glass memorial, flags, and murals. We took a picture of these, and we used it for one of our mass mailings. The outside world will never see it, only the victims' relatives. It was quite an emotional visit.

There is a wall of flags dedicated to the passengers of Flight #77 lining the hallway where the plane landed inside of the Pentagon walls. All of the flags were dedicated to the Pentagon by either schools or victims' families. We hear a lot about the memorial at ground zero, as well we should, but the memorial at the Pentagon is worthy of honorable mention. The engraved memorial benches that display each victim's name and birth date placed over a small stream of water is very calming. I'm grateful that someone put so much thought and care into this memorial. The beautiful tree that stands next to each bench, shadowing it from the glares of the sun, is breathtaking. The little golden pebbles that surround the benches from the youngest to the eldest are very tastefully done and will serve as a memorial as long as the hands of time permits its beauty to shine. We, the

Cottom family, are touched and truly grateful that Asia is part of this remembrance.

CHAPTER TWENTY-FOUR

The ASC Memorial Scholarship Fund

The Cottoms Share How the Legacy Began
www.asiacottom.com

The scholarship fund is where we have put our heart and passion. It is our story of tragedy to triumph. When it is all said and done, we still have the heart and passion to help others, and this is our triumph.

ASC Memorial Scholarship Fund Mission Statement

The Asia SiVon Cottom Memorial Scholarship Fund (ASC) was founded to honor the life of Asia SiVon Cottom. The fund's overall mission is to recognize and assist college students by providing financial assistance through scholarship awards to supplement financial obligations for tuition and educational fees. Scholarship awards will be made to deserving students who have excelled academically with special consideration given to students interested in math, science, and information technology.

ASC Memorial Scholarship Fund Vision

We honor the belief that a young person's character, when supported through education, is the foundation of the future. It is our vision that through this type of support, young people can receive quality education and, as a result, become productive citizens to our society.

The ASC is currently accepting corporate sponsorship and financial donations from individuals. To become a corporate sponsor or to make a personal donation, please visit the website at www.asiacottom.com.

The ASC Memorial Scholarship Fund is a non-profit 501(c)(3) organization. All contributions are tax-deductible to the full extent of the law.

**ASC Memorial Scholarship Fund
Attn: Regina Minor, Executive Director
5057 Sargent Road, Northeast
Washington, DC 20017**

* * *

Following the horrendous tragedy of Asia's passing during the 9/11 attacks, we felt a tremendous obligation to honor Asia in a way befitting a person of her spirit, intelligence, and love for learning. We founded the Asia SiVon Cottom (ASC) Memorial Scholarship Fund.

It was Nicole Green who first suggested we start a scholarship fund in Asia's name. She got it started for us and served as the first executive director. We were very interested, and I subsequently decided to write my dissertation on how to successfully manage a 501(c)(3) charity.

With financial contributions received from across the United States and internationally, we established the ASC Memorial Scholarship Fund in Asia's honor. Since the establishment of the fund, scholarships totaling approximately $85,000 have been awarded to deserving students, with the first award being presented in 2002. All donations raised from fundraisers are, and will be, used to make future scholarship awards. Our hope is that we can impact the lives of as many students as possible in honor of our precious daughter. Asia lives on through the endowment of each scholarship, touching lives still here on earth as she did for the entirety of her short eleven years.

We are so proud of each and every one of our ASC scholars. Their dedication to the furtherance of their education is evident in every aspect of their scholastic journey. The ASC Memorial Scholarship Fund is all about the young lives who are beneficiaries of the generosity of our faithful donors.

Asia loved learning and was particularly gifted in math, the sciences, and information technology. Her math and science magnet school, Bertie Backus Middle School, had state-of-the-art computer equipment and technology that gave her the opportunity to hone her exceptional computer skills. She had already completed two computer camp sessions the previous summer and was off to a great start at her first year in middle school.

She dreamed of one day becoming a pediatrician. The loss of our Asia was overwhelming, but we found some peace in affording deserving young students the opportunity to further their education.

A few days after 9/11 the American Red Cross initiated a 9/11 fund for the victims' families. Money came pouring in from concerned people from around the world. The donations that were made to the Red Cross were dispersed to families who suffered great losses of life during the 9/11 attacks. We not only received money, but we also received trinkets and knick knacks such as drawings, blankets, pillows, dolls, stuffed animals, plaques, cards, letters, tickets to events, flags, and a wishing well.

We were overwhelmed with the generosity of people and the heartfelt acts of sympathy from so many young people. Sometimes we would receive cash money and checks in the mail for eleven cents up to thousands of dollars at a time. The most heart-wrenching ones were the coin change we would receive from children with eleven cents symbolizing her eleven years of life. We received so much we couldn't house all of the gifts, so we started to give them away to people and places that held significance in Asia's life. We donated items and money to churches, schools, day cares, and business establishments that we frequented (e.g., Miller Copying Service, Beautiful One Hair Salon, and our church).

We are a tithing family, meaning we always give a percentage of our earnings to the church, as we ought to.

But, even this didn't seem like enough. We wanted to do something exceptional with the blessings we received.

Scholarship Fund

Once we adopt a scholar, our goal is to support him/her financially every year, for as long as he/she attends school and maintains a 3.0 grade point average. We currently have freshmen, sophomores, juniors, and seniors in our program. In the earlier years of the scholarship fund, we awarded the bulk of the money in the freshman year. Our focus was on people entering college and initially it was a "freshman scholarship." However, our scholars informed us that there are many avenues to obtain money through various scholarships for the first year, but if one continues with one's education, that is where the challenges lie. Now the initial award amount is given during the freshman year, and we continue to support the students throughout, but we award the bulk of the money to our upper classmen to help defray costs as they advance further in college.

Our dream is to award each ASC Scholar with a 100% scholarship, in other words a "full ride." We may have to change how we do things now, but that is my desire for the future ASC Scholarship Fund. Also, since the money is raised through donations and corporate sponsorships, we don't want the scholars to get a percentage of the proceeds; we want them to get it all.

As we move forward our ultimate goal is to move those on our advisory committee—who are really, in my mind, our seeds—to move them on to our executive board and to teach them how to run the fund. Eventually the fund will be Isiah's legacy. The role that Cottom and I play now as founders, Isiah will one day pick up the mantle and move the ASC Scholarship Fund into the future.

Regina Minor (my cousin) is currently our executive director. The future plan is for her daughter, India, to replace her when the time is right. She will assist her cousin Isiah in taking the ASC Scholarship Fund to the next level. Pastor Herbert Jackson currently serves on our executive board, and he is our press secretary. His children, Herbert Jr. and Whitney, will eventually take over his position(s) on the board.

Godchildren

Shortly after Asia died, Natalie Washington's parents asked me to become her godmother. Natalie and Asia were best friends ever since they were little girls. Natalie's father is the minister of music in our church and has been for over twenty-five years.

Paula Spruill and Erica Tanner (Toxan's sister) also asked me to be their godmothers. They were still young at the time, and each of them felt the loss of Asia as deeply as we do. I know they knew they couldn't replace Asia, but they all wanted me to continue to have a daughter. Those three young ladies will always hold a special place in my heart. Each of them gave me a Care Bear in different colors, each symbolizing their heart and love for me, and said they would always "care for me," just like Asia would have. Over the years Cottom and I have grown to love them all the more and spoiled them (according to their parents). In the spirit of giving each year, for birthdays and Christmas each young lady received a plethora of gifts all wrapped in their specific Care Bear color. Paula was pink, Natalie was purple, and Erica was orange. To this day, I continue to associate these colors with these young ladies. Later, India, Regina's daughter, also became one of my Care Bears. She was given the color yellow, and I probably spend more time with them than they spend with their parents. Sometimes when we go on family vacations the girls go with us, and we are all just one big happy family. Cottom is their godfather, and Isiah is their god-brother (which is why the ladies have a hard time trying to get around those girls. They are super protective of him, and he enjoys every bit of it).

When we originally started the scholarship fund, Paula and Toxan Tanner were the natural recipients because they were the ones who were in the church with Asia, and they were the first two to go to college. When we started to receive money from other places, we wanted to ensure there wouldn't be any favoritism. In order to maintain the fund's integrity, Cottom and I paid for our godchildren's student loans out of our own pockets, not from the ASC Scholarship Fund. We don't want our scholars to start out owing loans when they finish their education; that's why we want them to be debt free coming out of college. India is fortunate enough to have a college fund that was set aside for her. However, all of her college expenses are not covered. Subsequently, she is an ASC scholar.

Money

Following the 9/11 attacks, many law firms offered to represent us in filing a lawsuit against American Airlines. I wasn't interested in suing anyone. I was grieving, so I threw all of the solicitation packages into the trash.

On the contrary, during that time, American Airlines had sent a representative to our house to assist us with anything we needed. They brought my oldest brother home from Germany and paid for hotel space for my out-of-town relatives to attend Asia's memorial service. They paid for the funeral programs and brochures. Also, I believe they paid for Asia's headstone and ultimate interment. Then all of a sudden out of the blue, the kind gentlemen from American Airlines showed up at our doorstep and said, "From now on, *we will do as much as is necessary.*" This didn't sit too well with us.

The September 11th Victim Compensation Fund was created by an Act of Congress, the Air Transportation Safety and System Stabilization Act (49 USC 40101), shortly after 9/11 to compensate the victims of the attack (or their families) in exchange for their agreement not to sue the airline corporations involved. Kenneth Feinberg was appointed by Attorney General John Ashcroft to be Special Master of the fund. He worked for 33 months *and* developed the regulations governing the administration of the fund and administered all aspects of the program.

Feinberg was responsible for making the decisions on how much each family of a victim would receive. He had to estimate how much each victim would have earned in a full lifetime. If a family accepted the offer, it was not possible to appeal. Families unhappy with the offer were able to appeal in a non-adversarial, informal hearing to present their case however they wanted. Feinberg presided over more than 900 of the 1,600 hearings. At the end of the process, $7 billion was awarded to 97% of the families that opted into the fund, with an average payout of $1.8 million. A non-negotiable clause in the acceptance papers for the settlements stated that the families were to never file suit against the airlines for any lack of security or otherwise unsafe procedures.

A stumbling block to settlements was the fact that many of the World Trade Center victims were highly compensated financial professionals. Families of these victims felt the compensation offers were too low and, had a court considered their cases on an individual basis, they would have been awarded much higher amounts. This concern had to be balanced against the time, complications, and risks of pursuing an individual case, and the real possibility that the airlines and their insurers could be bankrupted before being able to pay the claim. The Victim's Fund used an economic formula to decide how to disperse the money from the fund.

The Victim's Fund was set up as a model to help families who have suffered catastrophic loss. The overall goal of the Fund is one of benevolence. However, what was missing was that fact that children were not accounted for; there was nothing included to compensate for the loss of a child because they didn't have any earning power at that time in their lives.

The 9/11 Victim Compensation Fund is based on the collateral source deductions. Simply stated, if we chose to receive money from the fund, the total amount of all life insurance money we received would be deducted from the amount allocated by the fund. Victims of 9/11 whom we talked to agreed with us: no one is clear on why that was a stipulation or how it is fair or equitable. It appears that responsible people (with life insurance) were penalized. If we were to receive compensation from the 9/11 Victim Compensation Fund for our loss, what difference would it make whether or not we received compensation from life insurance policies.

The family of Rodney Dickens, who was one of the other children on Flight #77 with Asia, was considering suing the airlines. It took some persuasion for me to agree to go ahead with a lawsuit. LaShawn Dickens suggested Mary Schiavo as the aviation attorney. Mary was working in California, so she flew to Washington, DC and sat at my dining room table. She informed me why she was passionate about this case. It was her passion and her heart that made us want to proceed with her firm.

When Mary entered Asia's room, she almost collapsed. Her daughter was six at the time, and Asia's bed looked exactly like her daughter's bed, including the same sheets. She said she felt overwhelmed with empathy for our pain because she imagined this could have been her own daughter who was taken away.

We wanted to show that every life should be valued as equal; one life is not worth more than another life, and that is what we wished to prove by launching the lawsuit. We wanted the children to be recognized and their families compensated.

If we are strictly working with charts, statistics, and laws of average, then Asia Cottom should not have been on Flight #77. As a young girl in the District of Columbia Public School (DCPS) system, the statistics say Asia should have been anything but a wonderful student and motivated scholar with special skills in computers, math, and science. Statistically speaking, there is no actuarial chart in the world that would predict that this little DCPS child would be selected by the National Geographic Society to go to California to complete marine research and, upon her return, write about her experiences so that other students may hear, read, and learn. What statistics couldn't see was that Asia set her personal standards very high and, even in her young life, always met them. Asia had ambitions to become a pediatrician. Given the fact that she always reached all of her goals, there was no reason to believe she wouldn't have become a pediatrician, just as she had hoped.

Asia's Name for Monetary Gain

It is important to understand that some people will use anything to gain an unfair advantage. Even though this is the case with Asia's fund, we still choose to pursue a "righteous path" and look to help and give to others.

Many people have tried, and are trying, to benefit from the notoriety of Asia's death. People used Asia's name for monetary gain through collecting donations using her name without our permission or knowledge and publishing work using Asia's name.

In one example, my mother, Pearl, saw a donation jar at a Laundromat with Asia's name on it. Neither Asia's family nor the fund set up in her name would benefit from those donations because we weren't even aware this money was being collected. In another example, a fund was set up for the DC Public Schools to collect money to benefit the children's families of 9/11. We are not affiliated with this organization, and we have not seen any money from it. Also products and trinkets are being sold using her name, including armbands. When people buy these items, they think they are benefiting the family or our organization, but this is not the case.

Nothing on the Internet with Asia's name on it has anything to do with our ASC Scholarship Fund, and we will not see any of that money. We have no idea who is behind these criminal acts. The only way to authentically donate money for her cause is through our website: www.asiacottom.com. I mention all of this so that readers can be wary of anything associated with Asia's name that is outside of the fund itself.

A Word of Caution

When we started to be blessed monetarily, some family, friends, and even some of the people that we went to church with every day viewed us differently. I am still unclear how you can be jealous or envious of other people's blessings, especially when they were blessed through pain.

The money didn't change us; it changed the people around us. We are the same people we always were.

We received a reasonable settlement so the first thing we did was tithe. We also paid for other children's educations, gave money to family, to entities, and to ministries that aren't even part of the New Smyrna Missionary Baptist Church. We were tithers and givers prior to Asia's passing, so we continued to donate money as we always had.

The money we received we see as a gift from God, because we didn't have to get anything. People lose children every day, and they aren't financially compensated. We received insurance money from National Geographic, the settlement money from American Airlines, and as responsible adults we had a life insurance policy on Asia. It has been our privilege to give whenever and wherever we can. While *nothing* can replace our child, giving to others allows us to remember Asia in positive ways.

The gospel singer, CeCe Winans, wrote a song with the following line in it: "You don't know the cost of the oil in the alabaster box." God has blessed us with a financial "alabaster box." However, it was costly – the price of a child. We would give every cent back to God or away to others, if it would bring our child home to us. But that is not going to happen. So we cannot be ashamed of what God has given us. And I had to learn that from Cottom. I wasn't a miser or cheap, or anything like that, but I thoughtfully considered what I bought or did because I was concerned how other people would view it. Cottom taught me how to learn to enjoy God's blessings. Bishop helped me too.

Once we had tithed, donated money to the causes we believed in, and gave money away, we talked about what we wanted to buy. We decided we would buy a car because we shared an automobile.

Cottom said, "Why don't we buy a Mercedes Benz, just like Asia wanted?" I had often talked with Asia about dream cars. Hers was a burgundy Mercedes Benz with grey interior.

I said, "We can't do that."

He said, "Well, this is how much it costs, and we have the money."

The first thing I said was, "But what are people going to think?"

He said, "Well, damn what the people think."

I thought to myself, *Well they are going to talk about me if I buy a car, and they are going to talk about me if I don't.* At the end of the day, Cottom was right.

So, we went to a car dealership. We walked into the showroom and a car that looked exactly as Asia had described it was on display. Burgundy exterior with a grey interior! We bought the car, and we also bought a license plate for that car with the letters ASIA on it. To this day, my car still has her tag on it.

Fundraisers

We tried to have fundraisers every year, but the workload became too burdensome for our volunteers. It is a lot of work, and it takes many volunteers to successfully manage a fundraiser. However, all of the volunteers on the executive board are motivated and willing to work hard to make the scholarship fund a success.

This can only be done with sufficient donations and volunteers.

Fundraisers to Date

Our very first fundraiser was a Gospel Extravaganza in our church. We invited a bunch of local churches and their dance ministries to perform. We had a great time with at least 300 people in attendance. We took a free-will offering from the attendees and after our expenses were paid, our profit was $5,000. We were so excited we were able to pay for books and award a few more scholarships that next fall semester.

On what would have been Asia's 22nd birthday, Cottom held a basketball tournament. It started around Christmas time and finished on January 13th, her birthday. We had special t-shirts made that said, "Happy Birthday Asia." The number 22 was on the sleeve. The basketball players wore them over their uniforms.

We held a bike ride fundraiser for several years. Asia loved biking, so this was our motivation to do a fundraiser of this nature. We charged $50, and half of that went to payment for a t-shirt with Asia's logo, a backpack, and a water bottle, and the other half went directly to the scholarship fund.

We've sponsored jazz auctions and solicited funds through corporate mailings. We are always looking for new and exciting ways to raise funds for our scholars. Our hope is to sponsor a celebrity golf tournament in the coming year. We also sponsored a line dance party fundraiser. We had t-shirts for this as well.

Every time we organize a function we have what I like to call paraphernalia for sale: pens, water bottles, Asia pins, and t-shirts. These continue to be sold on Asia's website. All proceeds, minus the direct costs, go directly to the scholarship fund.

CHAPTER TWENTY-FIVE

Scholarship Essays and Awards

Scholarship Essays

Paula Spruill: Part of the qualifying process for an ASC Memorial Fund Scholarship is writing an essay about how the 9/11 attacks affected the potential recipient and how their educational aspirations and future career path are a response to that experience.

In addition to filling out an application form that is available on our website, students must complete an essay to be considered for a scholarship. In the early days of the scholarship fund, students were asked to write about how 9/11 affected them. But the new generation of students graduating from high school weren't old enough to even remember 9/11, let alone write about it. So, we're coming up with new essay questions for the applicants. This new phase of the scholarship fund, apart from the impact of 9/11, is difficult because, for me, the Asia SiVon Cottom Memorial Scholarship Fund was always all about 9/11. It is challenging to come up with an essay question that doesn't have anything to do with the scope and influence of that tragedy.

The following are a sampling of essays written by scholarship applicants over the years:

Essay by Akilah Grimes – 2011

I can still remember the day that September 11th occurred. I was only twelve years old at the time, but I remember coming home from school and realizing that something was wrong. My parents turned on the T.V. and I could not believe what I saw; it was like a scene out of a movie. I could not help but feel sorrow inside, even at a young age, because I knew that this was something that should not have happened. People's lives were lost, including Asia's, for a reason beyond our control as American citizens.

Now that it is ten years later, there have been many changes to the way society handles everyday actions including security measures and people's perception of foreigners. Due to this tragic incident, security levels and alerts have been at an all-time high. There are extra precautions in the airport, and when certain events are taking place that involve high-ranking officers such as the president, there are even more in place. These changes came about to try and help America combat any future incidents from happening, but it still puts a lot of people on edge. People no longer feel safe in their own country, and they also do not trust that they are being properly protected. There is only so much the government can do without violating people's privacy.

In relation to people's perception, an event like this would, of course, alter how people view others from the Middle East. Even though that is stereotyping, because of what occurred these kinds of thoughts were going to arise and are still present to this day. A friend of mine just told me the other day that he was flying and was sitting beside a person of Middle Eastern descent and wanted to move because he thought he was a terrorist. This was unfair to the man because he did not do anything to deserve this treatment, but this was all in reaction to September 11th, which happened ten years ago.

In the future I want to be a doctor, and I was made aware that Asia wanted to be one too. I feel as if by becoming a physician, I would be able to touch a number of people's lives and ultimately help them. I can assist in times of turmoil in the future which hopefully will be few and far between. I can use my profession to better society like Asia would have done. It is very unfortunate that Asia was on that flight because she was on it for a positive reason. Everything happens for a reason though, and what we must do as a society, and as Americans, is learn from the incident and ultimately make a change. We need to be more aware of our policies and how we come off to other countries so peace may be in the world, not war. It is only right that we strive to better ourselves, and I can personally do this by becoming a doctor.

Essay by Ashley Benson – "How 9/11 Changed Me"

Like many in the United States, the events of September 11, 2001 came as a complete shock to me. On the news, I remember seeing giant-sized towers meekly tumbling to the ground. I remember seeing the impenetrable Pentagon being defeated by a simple airplane. I remember tens of thousands of innocent lives lost, and families and friends forever traumatized on that day. I also remember thinking about the people who still had so much to accomplish and even more to enjoy in life. Thinking about all this made me reminisce on the sad fact that I was one of those friends who lost someone that day.

I was in the 6th grade when it happened. All of my classmates and I were studying reading comprehension when, one by one, people began to get called to the office. In less than twenty minutes, there were ten students left out of a class of twenty-five. Rumors quickly spread about where everyone had gone. People spoke of mass doctor appointments, a random assembly, and just about anything else one could think of. The next name called over the PA system was my own. My mother was coming to take me home. Very soon I learned that the World Trade Center Towers and the Pentagon were hit in a terrorist attack.

A few hours later I was told more shocking news. I found out, just like many others, that someone dear to me was a victim of this attack. My friend, Asia Cottom, was killed in the attack on the Pentagon. My heart sank. I could not believe that this could happen to someone so close to me. I started to think of all the times we played together and all the times we joked and laughed. I thought about how we talked about all the things we would do when we got older. My friend was gone.

The memories of that day have motivated me to do the best that I can while I am still in this world. They have pushed me to do the things Asia and I talked about achieving throughout our lives. They have motivated me to make a positive and lasting impression within my community by setting an example for African-American females. I strive to continue my education through college in order to reach my goals. Attending and succeeding in college will show other Black females in my community that they should not submit to the terrible stereotypes that are associated with their race, including the stereotype that Black females are uneducated and lazy. When I receive my degree in Communication Arts from Johnson C. Smith University, I will not only pursue my career in public relations, but also in communicating the importance of pursuing a college education.

Essay by Brittany Woodfolk – "Personal Statement"

The September 11th attacks that took place in 2001 tragically affected the entire nation. I remember sitting in third period in Mrs. Davis' class at Walton Middle School when an announcement was made over the intercom. With an uneasy tone in his voice, Principal Huan encouraged all of the teachers to turn on the news. Every student, including myself, was puzzled and completely unaware of the situation. After hearing the frantic reports of the newscasters and viewing the treacherous collapse of the Twin Towers of the World Trade Center and the Pentagon, I felt helpless. But at that very moment I did realize that there was one thing I could do—I could pray for all of the people affected by this ordeal.

A few teachers and close friends of mine had family members pass away that day. My heart was so heavy and hurting for each and every person involved. But this was a chance to offer sympathy, compassion, and support to my friends. Since that day, many teachers and students joined together to promote a place of encouragement and optimism by making cards and posters, taking a moment of silence at the beginning of class, and uplifting our peers.

Today's society is still very much shaped by the occurrences from September 11th; there were both physical and emotional scars. For instance, many of the rescue and recovery workers currently suffer from debilitating illnesses from the 2,500 contaminants of that day. People risked their lives in order to save another life. Emotionally, the attacks on the Pentagon and the Twin Towers were a harsh reality—bringing shock, fear, dismay, and confusion. But now, each year, this day is set aside to reflect and honor the victims and their loved ones. One of my favorite memorials is that of the Pentagon Memorial, which was completed and opened to the *public on September 11, 2008. Asia is one of the 184 victims on America Airlines Flight #77 that this memorial is dedicated to.*

Hearing Asia SiVon Cottom's story has greatly inspired me. I am sure she felt honored to be selected as one of the three students to attend the National Geographic Oceanic Exploration. At just eleven years old, which was also my age at the time, she had already taken the initiative to explore and take on a new adventure. I have no doubt that, if given the opportunity, she would have had a huge impact on her community and those around her.

I plan to greatly impact my community, and the world, through my education, talents, skills, passion, etc. Taking advantage of the opportunities at the University of Virginia has helped me to grow and mature mentally, spiritually, and emotionally. One way that U.V. has helped me is by broadening my perspective on possible career paths in sociology. Sociology is the study of human social behavior, and this field amazes me how people interact with one another and how they adapt to their environment. This social science field is complimentary to the "hard" sciences, like mathematics. Not only do scientists and mathematicians perform experiments and collect data, but sociologists must do the same. In sociology one attempts to observe phenomena that interest him or her, and then he or she collects and analyzes data. For instance, my current research proposal examines the effects that tracking and labeling kindergarten students has on their educational performance and how it influences their self-perception. Once I have my results, I am able to interpret how the information reflects the educational system. I want to use my feelings to better the local schools and give awareness to the positive and negative aspects of tracking and labeling.

Another reason why sociology is important is because it can influence the development of new technology and procedures. Last year, as summer intern at the Office of Emergency Preparedness at the University of Virginia, I helped with organizing the university's first large-scale stadium evacuation exercise. This accomplishment turned out to be a huge success, and my supervisor told me that other departments began to take more secure measures in preparing for hazardous situations. Unfortunately, one of the reasons why so many people in the World Trade Center did not make it out of the towers was because the evacuation plan was not strongly implemented. The September 11th attacks were one of the incidents that inspired us to execute and put into operation our evacuation exercise.

Lastly, I value every chance I have to help fellow students, family, church, and community members. I have a strong passion for working with and strengthening children and families. One of the organizations I am currently involved in is YWLP (Young Women Leaders Program), a mentoring program empowering middle school girls to be leaders at school and in their community. It has motivated me to start a Christian mentoring program for grades 7–12 at Evergreen Ministries. Although I do not know the job title or occupation I want to have, I am certain that I will continue to engage myself in the affairs and concerns of my family, school, church, and community.

Essay by India L. Minor – "September 11, 2001"

On September 11, 2001, I was in the 4th grade sitting in class at my current school, Riverdale Baptist. I remember parents arriving early to pick up their kids at 11 a.m. instead of the normal dismissal time of 3 p.m. I did not know what was going on. When my mother arrived to pick me up, I asked her why everybody was leaving the school. Even after she gave me an explanation, I still did not know what was happening at the time.

My mother and I were watching the news reports of the plane crashing into a building in New York. I was confused because the news was showing the Pentagon, yet the news reporters were talking about New York. I did not realize the significance of what happened until I was eleven years old from various class discussions. I felt sad for all the innocent people that were hurt and lost their lives.

A few years passed before I knew that my cousin, Asia Cottom, was on the infamous American Airlines Flight #77 plane that was hijacked and redirected to hit the Pentagon. She was en route to California on a field trip sponsored by National Geographic. She was selected to participate in one of the nation's premier undersea projects. I regret that I did not get a chance to meet her and grow up with a cousin whom I have so much in common. As I got older, I realized that something should have been done to catch the people who caused the horrific damages. To me it seems like very little was done. I feel that the United States' reaction was not swift enough. But, some of the culprits are still being caught, convicted, and charged today.

My parents agreed to keep me enrolled in private school to get the best educational foundation. Unfortunately, I had to lose my father at an early age. Getting used to being without my father's physical presence is the significant challenge in my life. But, I still feel his strength and encouragement. Because of the significant sacrifices that my mother has endured over the past ten years as a single parent, my goal is to honor my father by studying for a bachelor's degree at a major university in the state of Maryland. I enjoy talking with kids to help develop their communication skills and to strengthen their confidence to help solve personal problems. Because of this interest, I am also contemplating the Social Service Track in the Criminal Justice major. I would like to volunteer as a mentor. In addition, I would hope to meet students from other states and countries to enhance my social and educational development.

If I am chosen to receive the scholarship that was established in memory of someone that I still desire to know so much about, "the girl with the big smile," this would give me an opportunity to excel at my dreams in her memory. It would be a challenge, an honor, and my pleasure to further my education with the aspiration of carrying Asia with me and making her proud.

Essay by Jeremiah Harring

On September 11, 2001, it was a very sad day for millions of people in America. I was very young and didn't understand what was going on. The only thing my 3rd grade class was told was that a plane hit a building and a lot of people were injured. I didn't understand what had really happened until I was a little older. I thought someone my teacher knew had gotten hurt. Her response was, "No it's not that, it's the simple fact that something tragic has happened unexpectedly." She expressed so much compassion for the families that were affected by this tragedy. It affected my grandmother and now that I am older I understand the impact of that event is not easy to deal with when it's tragic and unexpected.

Community/World—there are a lot of students and even more kids who are pregnant these days and many kids these days with more to come. I would be an understanding teacher that kids can come to for any types of problems or issues, and I will be there to have their back because I was once in their shoes and didn't understand a lot. Now I can help them because I know the feeling.

My life has been impacted from the events of 9/11 with the implementation of tighter security. Not to say America didn't have security, but now it's strongly enforced everywhere you go. The articles I have read about the 9/11 attack state that people suffered post-traumatic stress disorder. I now believe this is what happened to my teacher and grandmother. Again, I was too young to truly comprehend what had happened. One article mentioned that this attack was the largest on US soil. I am not fearful, but some people are still fearful of another attack since this attack happened just out of the blue. However, after reading articles about the attack I can understand the reason for tighter security.

As a Business Education Major I will learn how to assist in making the US a safer and more educated place to live. I would first start in my community by volunteering to educate kids on how to love themselves, to be leaders and not followers. If you see a friend doing something wrong, encourage them to stop and don't go along with what they are doing wrong. Doing wrong at a young age will only lead to doing wrong at an older age. This will put you at risk of being just like the people who attacked the US on 9/11. I would encourage people to take advantage of all the opportunities that are available to improve their lives. Get your education and don't play around like I did my first two years of high school. Your life is determined by the choices you make. Always make the right choice, think twice before you do things, and you will succeed; and when you succeed don't forget where you came from and help someone else improve their life.

Essay by Marielle Eldridge

September 11, 2001 was the beginning of first grade and was also my mother's birthday. I remember being picked up early and not knowing why, but not thinking much of it. I don't recall much after that day, but I do know that it heavily impacted not only those in the United States, but the whole world. Since 9/11, my life has been impacted in knowing that my mother's birthday will always fall on the day of the tragic events of 9/11. It has also made a major impact on traveling. Recently I took a trip to Atlanta; my mother and I had a scheduled flight for 9:45 a.m. and we arrived at the airport at 8:30 a.m. We believed that we would be able to make our flight on time. The plane was still at the gate, but they told us that they had completed their final head count. We had to wait to take a later flight. Although my mother and I were a bit upset by this, we understood that the airport and airline service provider were doing their part to protect and secure their passengers. This is a direct result of the enhanced protective measures put in place after 9/11.

As I prepare for my first year of college I'd like to achieve my goals. As a biology/pre-med major I am working towards becoming a reconstructive plastic surgeon. I chose this profession because I would love to help people, especially those who have gone through traumatic events like soldiers or other victims. Being able to help those feel good and comfortable with themselves through surgery is something that I would love to do. I would like to help those who are also under-privileged in the community and throughout the world live a better life.

First Recipients of the ASC Memorial Scholarship Fund

Paula Spruill

My name is Paula Spruill, and I was the first scholarship recipient of The Asia SiVon Cottom (ASC) Memorial Scholarship Fund, before the current program was even in place. I am so grateful for the opportunity to pursue the career path that I have chosen, and I look forward to giving back through the scholarship fund. When it came to me pursuing my professional law degree, the ASC Memorial Fund was of tremendous benefit since tuition is usually about $32,000 to $37,000 a year plus living expenses. Even one year of tuition that expensive is a huge financial strain! Without the help of the scholarship fund, I can say with confidence that I would not be where I am today.

It all started with a bright young girl named Asia. I knew Asia Cottom because both of our families attended the same church led by our pastor, Dr. Earl A. Ross. Right before my senior year in high school, her father approached me about helping Asia with reading. At the time, I was seventeen and she was ten. Both Asia and I loved math, but we both hated reading. We could do math problems, but we didn't care for an arithmetic problem that was written out in paragraph form. Word problems—NOT our favorite!

From the fall of 2000 to early spring of 2001, I would go pick her up from her home and then bring her over to my house. At that time we lived right around the corner from each other. We would read through a book, and I would help her with certain words she needed help understanding, and then I would bring her back home.

As an engineering student, books are expensive, especially because you may not be able to find them used. I was blessed because my parents were able to put me through college; our agreement was that they would pay for tuition and room and board, and I would be responsible for my spending money and books. I also had other scholarships to help out. At that time I didn't have to complete an essay like scholarship applicants have to do now. When 9/11 happened I was just starting college as an engineering student. I qualified for the scholarship because I was pursuing an engineering degree, and the scholarship was intended to be of assistance to those interested in math, science, and technology. I received my first scholarship from the ASC Memorial Scholarship Fund in the spring of 2002, the second semester of my first year. It mostly paid for my books.

Because of the scholarship fund, I didn't have to choose my career path based on requisite income I needed to live and also repay law school loans plus interest for my tuition and living expenses. New doors opened up for me because of the help I received. It has truly made a difference in my life. Recently I started volunteering on the executive board to give back in a tangible way. We are all volunteers. The other members of the executive board are Clifton Cottom, Dr. Michelle Cottom, Dr. Pastor Herbert Jackson, and Regina Minor.

The executive board is in the process of brainstorming ideas for fundraisers. In the past we have had an auction, a bike ride, and a soul line dance party. We are hoping to have a concert around 9/11 this year. We have talked about new ways to bring in funds so that we can have a greater impact here in Washington, DC and across the nation. Every time there is an event for the ASC Memorial Scholarship Fund, family and friends of the executive board help out in the planning. I currently work for Duke University's Duke Clinical Research Institute, but I always come home for any event for the scholarship. It is a privilege to serve in any way I can.

Initially the fund was only set up to help those in their freshman years. Fortunately, my parents didn't have to pay anything for the first year of college because of the scholarships I had received. After that first year, most of my scholarships just dropped off. The dream of Clifton and Michelle Cottom is to be able to pay for the college students through their college years and not just for the freshman year. There is a tremendous need for students to receive assistance in their latter years of college.

Another goal of the ASC Memorial Scholarship Fund executive board is to work on building up the scholarship. In the past it has been just a word of mouth kind of thing, but we are definitely considering ways we can develop it with more individual and corporate donations.

The greater the reach of the scholarship fund, the larger the impact we can make in the lives of deserving young people across the country.

Update on Paula Spruill

Paula Spruill, J.D. – ASC Memorial Scholarship Recipient. Paula Spruill received her bachelor of science degree in industrial and systems engineering as well as a business minor from Virginia Tech in Blacksburg, VA in May 2006. She continued her studies at the University of New Hampshire Law School (formerly the Franklin Pierce Law Center) in Concord, New Hampshire, earning a Juris Doctor in May 2009.

The first recipient of the ASC Memorial Scholarship Fund, Paula Spruill is a native of Washington, DC. During her time at Virginia Tech, Paula was the first

African-American to be appointed as Chief Justice of the Virginia Tech Undergraduate Honor System. Paula also mentored first year African-American and female engineering students and was actively involved with the National Society of Black Engineers' Pre-College Initiative program for high school students in southwest Virginia.

While attending University of New Hampshire School of Law, Ms. Spruill was an active member in her local Black Law Students Association (BLSA) chapter. She also served on a committee of students dedicated to the retention of minority students as well as increasing diversity. During the 2008–2009 academic year, Paula served as the Northeast Black Law Students Association (NEBLSA) regional secretary and was awarded the honor of Most Outstanding NEBLSA Executive Board Member.

Upon graduating from law school in May 2009, Paula worked for the University of Virginia as a senior contract negotiator. She now works as a contracts associate for Duke University's Duke Clinical Research Institute.

Toxan Tanner – ASC Memorial Scholarship Second Recipient

Graduating from Largo High School in Largo, MD in 2002, Toxan Tanner completed her undergraduate study at Howard University in Washington, DC. She earned her bachelor of science in psychology with a human development minor in May 2006. She then went on to earn her Master of Arts degree in teaching and elementary education from Trinity College in Washington, DC.

While at Howard University, she worked with Heads Up: A University Initiative, a tutoring program teaching literacy in area DC public schools. It was with this program that Toxan realized that she wanted to be a literacy specialist working in urban public schools. Toxan graduated in May 2006 and continued with Heads Up through Spring 2007. In the fall of 2007 she began graduate school to obtain her master's in teaching for elementary education from Trinity College in Washington, DC.

Toxan is currently entering her fifth year as an elementary school teacher in the Washington, DC area. For four years, she taught second grade and will be teaching third grade science in the coming school year. As an educator, it is her goal to enlighten students to the power of education and to give them the tools to become free thinkers and for learning to become an infectious and lifelong mainstay within their lives. The ASC scholarship was helpful for Toxan to attain her academic goals. With the help of their scholarship, she was able to focus on her studies without having to consider the financial struggle. She was also continuously motivated by fellow educators and members of the ASC Memorial Scholarship Fund to not give up and continue to push forward as she attained her master's degree and began teaching.

April S. Harvey – ASC Memorial Scholarship Third Recipient

April Harvey of Elyria, Ohio graduated from Howard University in Washington, DC with a bachelor's of science degree in sports medicine and a minor in chemistry in June 2009. She had the distinct honor of graduating magna cum laude, with a 3.5 cumulative grade point average. During her tenure, she served as both vice president and president of the National Society of Collegiate Scholars, secretary and vice president of the Howard University Ohio Club, community service chair of the National Council of Negro Women, Howard University Section, and fundraising coordinator of the Howard University Alumni Association of Cleveland. She volunteered with the Bethlehem Rebounders (feeding homeless individuals within the DC Community), the American Diabetes Association, along with serving as the program coordinator for the Dinner Program for Homeless Women. Ms. Harvey served as a volunteer with the 2009 Presidential Inauguration Committee and was also a 2009 inductee of the Who's Who among Students in American Colleges and Universities. Furthermore, she served as an intern for the Washington Wizards 2007-2008 season in the Community Relations department. At Howard, she received the Nellie M. Quander Memorial Scholarship, Howard University Trustee Scholarship, and the Mary Rose Reeves Allen Endowed Scholarship.

Following her undergraduate studies, April relocated to Atlanta, Georgia, where she now works in marketing and advertising.

"I am so thankful to have been a recipient of the ASC Memorial Scholarship. When I was a junior in high school, I was offered the opportunity of a lifetime to attend the National Student Leadership Conference at Johns Hopkins University in Baltimore, MD. The NSLC invites a select group of outstanding high school students to participate in its fast-paced, high-level, interactive summer sessions in the professional field of the student's choice. I was very excited for the opportunity to attend but unfortunately could not afford the admission costs. As I began to search for resources along with my parents, I applied for the ASC Memorial Scholarship and was awarded a scholarship that covered my costs to attend. It was an absolutely amazing, profound, and rewarding experience that would not have been possible without the ASC Memorial Scholarship Fund. Furthermore, the ASC Memorial Scholarship also provided assistance during my post-secondary education at Howard University.

I am very grateful and blessed to have been chosen as a recipient of the scholarship. As a token of appreciation, I now serve as the assistant to the executive director of the ASC Memorial Scholarship Fund and have done so since September of 2005. I am excited for the opportunity to assist others with post-education expenses, as the fund has helped me."

Ashley Benson – ASC Memorial Scholarship Recipient 2008/2009

Though Ashley Benson is just starting out as a freshman at Johnson C. Smith University in Charlotte, North Carolina, she has achieved many accomplishments. These accomplishments range from earning filmmaking awards to making the dean's list in college. During high school, Ashley earned an award for

"Excellence in Filmmaking" in the field of historic research on her documentary focused on the Vietnam War draft resistance. Ashley has also received the 2007 Panasonic Kid Witness News Award for Best Documentary for the same film entitled *We Will Not Fight: Draft Resistance in the Vietnam War.* In addition to this award, Ashley has received the ASC Memorial Scholarship in 2008/2009. During her first year of college Ashley Benson has achieved the distinction of the dean's list with a GPA of 3.4. Ashley is also a member of the National Society of Collegiate Scholars.

Ashley Benson Update

One of our ASC Memorial Scholarship recipients and an alumna of Johnson C. Smith University, Ashley Benson, has benefited greatly from the scholarship fund. Since receiving the ASC Memorial Scholarship in 2008 and 2009, Ashley was able to complete her undergraduate education, with a B.A. in communication arts. During her undergraduate career, the scholarship fund has allowed her the means to appreciate charitable organizations and recognize the great things the scholarship fund does for the community.

Since her freshman year, Ashley Benson has earned dean's list, become a proud member of Sigma Gamma Rho Sorority, Incorporated, and is still a member of the National Society of Collegiate Scholars. The collaborative impacts of these organizations, as well as the ASC Memorial Scholarship Fund, have deeply grounded Ashley in the greater good and the motivation such organizations put forth in the community.

Lawrence J. B. Pulliam – ASC Memorial Scholarship Recipient 2008/2009

Lawrence J.B. Pulliam presently attends Montgomery College in Rockville, Maryland. His major is Computer Gaming and Simulation with a focus upon Game Production. Lawrence Pulliam is also in the transfer program with the University of Baltimore at Shady Grove. Upon receiving his associate of arts degree from Montgomery College, he will transition to the UMBC (University of Maryland Baltimore County) program the fall of 2010. There, he will work towards a bachelor of science in simulation and digital entertainment. His GPA is 3.24, and he was a 2008/2009 recipient of an ASC Memorial Scholarship.

Lawrence Pulliam Update 2013/2014

I am Lawrence Pulliam, a student at the University of Baltimore. I earned my associates of arts degree from Montgomery College in 2010 and am currently applying for graduation and my bachelor of the arts degree from the University of Baltimore, with the search for a place of employment already underway as well. Throughout, ASC has been a constant support system and benefit to me in all of my academic endeavors, be they financial or mental. The scholarship fund has been a blessing for me in aiding me in times of need and keeping me encouraged and motivated. I can truly say that without ASC, I may not have made it this far.

Jeremiah Harrington

Garrett College, 2014 – A.A., Business Administration

Frostburg University, 2016

Jeremiah Harrington – 2011 graduate of Spingarn Senior High School. In the fall of 2011,

I was a proud freshman at Garrett College in McHenry, Maryland. I will be the first male in my entire family to attend college, and my family and I are very excited.

I'm proud to be going off to college and making my family proud. The major I am pursuing is Business Management/Computer Technology because I love math, and becoming an accountant would be perfect for me. But I also have a passion for computers. I find them so interesting and fun to work with, and I think becoming a computer technician would also be great for me. So I'm still contemplating on a final major decision.

Currently, I am a junior at Frostburg State University and my major is accounting. In May 2014, I graduated from Garrett College with a 3.2 GPA and my A.A. in Business Administration. The Asia Cottom Memorial Scholarship helps me in many ways. The background and sole foundation of the scholarship encourages me to be the best I am and never take life for granted because you never know how long you have it for. It also motivates me to do my best academically to continue to receive the help and support from the scholarship committee.

Keturah Wallace

Johnson C. Smith University 2016

My name is Keturah Wallace, currently a junior attending Johnson C. Smith University in Charlotte, North Carolina, studying the science of chemistry, with an ultimate

goal of becoming a forensic scientist. I am aware that a degree in chemistry could lead me to many opportunities such as lab research and development, but I plan to pursue forensic science so that I can assist the criminal justice systems in not just convicting but also exonerating persons through forensic science. I have always understood how important it is to live a law-abiding life, and with a chemistry degree I can assist the law enforcement community through forensic science.

My interest in chemistry was enhanced after meeting the executive director of the Metropolitan Police Firearm and Fingerprinting, Ms. Karen A. Wiggins on November 24, 2010. I had visited various departments under her supervision at the Metropolitan Police Department of Washington DC headquarters. I was allowed to meet and interact with the staff of the Firearms and Fingerprint Examination Division. I enjoyed assisting an officer with the test firing of two weapons. I was instructed on how the firing pin of the shell casing of each weapon fired left a distinct marking. I was also shown how the bullet would have a distinct imprint after traveling through the barrel of a gun. I was also able to visit the fingerprint section and assist lab techs as they would operate on an ordinary day.

Ms. Wiggins is intelligent and thorough. She explained the college courses I would need to advance in the forensic field. I was told the purpose behind excelling in math and science courses. I would not be as interested in science as I am now without her guidance. Fortunately, I was able to obtain a research internship the summer of 2013. This research gave me experience in a laboratory, as well as experience with scientific instruments.

Now attending a four-year university, it is my desire to obtain a bachelor's of science degree in chemistry. Following, I plan to attend graduate school to obtain a master's degree and potentially a doctorate and, with dedication and support, I shall succeed.

Update on Keturah Wallace

"As a past recipient, the ASC Scholarship has helped me and my education tremendously. I was awarded dean's list for two semesters at my university. I have also been accepted as a participant of a Research Experience for Undergraduate (REU) students at Virginia Commonwealth University. This summer will complete two summers of research experience that ultimately helps me in excelling in my field of study, chemistry. Entering the fall 2014 at Johnson C. Smith University, I will be a junior. With two years of college complete, I am excited and ready for any challenges that may come."

Asia SiVon Cottom Memorial Scholarship Fund
Current Recipients Testimonials

M. Eldridge (Fisk University, 2016)

My first year at Fisk has been wonderful. Upon completing my first year, I have made many new friends as well as had many opportunities to serve the community and strive academically. Although biology was a challenge, I really enjoyed the challenge and hope to stay motivated and work even harder to do better in my upcoming courses.

I was accepted into the Leadership Enrichment and Academic Development program also known as LEAD. I also earned the emerging leader award. I am also a part of the DC, Maryland, and Virginia Club, as well as the International/Caribbean Club.

Upon returning to Fisk for the fall semester, I will be an orientation leader, which means I will be welcoming the new freshman class of 2017 on the campus, as well as guiding them and helping them along the way. I am also going to join the track and field team. I am so very thankful for this scholarship, and how it has inspired me to do the best I can academically.

Niya Lewis, Hampton University, 2013

Niya Lewis is a graduate of Hampton University. She graduated with a bachelor's of arts degree in psychology. During her tenure at Hampton, she was an active member in the Student Government Association (SGA), NAACP, NCNW, and the Psychology Club. She is currently participating in the federal pathways program as an intern and was offered a full-time position post-graduation. Niya will be attending graduate school at Bowie State University seeking a master's degree in counseling psychology. Niya aspires to pursue her doctorate in clinical psychology and work with a diverse population of people.

Nylah Burton, Howard University, 2016

After being homeschooled by my mother for my whole life, I was accepted to many colleges and universities, including Howard University, the University of Virginia–Charlottesville, the University of Maryland–College Park, and Wake Forest University. I decided to attend Howard University on an academic scholarship and chose to major in political science and minor in Arabic language. While homeschooled, I started a service project called Traveling

Grace, which distributes duffel bags filled with sundry items to foster children in Prince George's County.

Currently, I am continuing my studies at Howard University, where my concentration in political science is international relations. This summer, I am also going on a research trip to Turkey and Greece. So far, I have really enjoyed my time at Howard. It has been a wonderful to learn about so many different cultures and to be around such a rich African-American heritage that is unique to an HBCU (Historically Black Colleges and Universities). I really want to thank you for your generosity.

* * *

Recipients of ASC Scholarship Fund listed by year

All of the deserving young people who have benefited from the generosity of the ASC Memorial Scholarship Fund founders and donors are doing their part to make the world a better place, one community, one school, one child at a time. Their dreams and aspirations are a living tribute to Asia Cottom and the bright future that she most certainly would have achieved.

2013 Recipients

- Nylah Burton – Freshman – Howard University
- Nykia Shepard – Freshman – Stevenson University

- Keturah Wallace – Freshman – Johnson C. Smith University

2012 Recipient

- Marielle Eldridge – Freshman – Fisk University

2011 Recipient

- Akilah Grimes – Graduate Student – Hampton University (B.S., biology), 2011 East Carolina University

2010 Recipients

- Herbert Jackson III – Freshman – Virginia Union University (2015 expected)
- Milton Jenkins – Freshman – Shaw University
- India Minor – Freshman – Towson University (December 2014 expected, B.A. deaf studies)
- Brittany Woodfolk – Junior – University of Virginia

2009 Recipients

- Niya Lewis – Hampton University (2013, B.A. psychology)

2008 Recipient

- Lawrence J.B. Pulliam – Montgomery College (2010, A.A. simulation and digital entertainment)

- University of Baltimore – Shady Grove (2010, ongoing, B.A. media design and animation)
- Ashley Benson – John C. Smith (2012, B.A. communications)

CHAPTER TWENTY-SIX

Accepting What God Allows

Michelle's Personal Journey of Healing

As you read the following, I want to share a journey of healing. While you may not believe in God the way my family and I do, I hope you can still glean insights into your own path of healing, or help someone who is in need of healing.

Before and after Asia's passing, I was frontline in a church that is well known for our healing and deliverance ministry. I was on the worship team and in a place of leadership. The trouble was, I was *supposed* to have the gift of healing and answers on how to help heal others, but I didn't. Just because death is inevitable, does it mean it is fair in our minds? And death that comes via anything other than natural causes, how can any of us consider that fair? My very soul was grieving, and my heart felt like someone had opened my chest and ripped it to shreds; I was in pain, and I couldn't find healing, not even in my own church.

Everyone is Different

A person's heart is a delicate thing, and we all grieve, question, change, heal, cope, and even grow during different times, different seasons, and in different ways. We are all unique, and we must respect that uniqueness. But people were looking to me for answers that made sense of what happened to my family and me—and maybe even answers to their own struggles. I simply didn't have them. Even though I spent huge amounts of time speaking with my immediate and extended family, not to mention my church family, co-workers, neighbors and Asia's friends, I really and truly didn't have the answers that would bring me any comfort. It didn't matter because the questions kept coming, and I had to respond. There were interview requests from radio, TV, and magazines all pressing me for answers.

Nevertheless, I continued with my studies in divinity, partly because I knew it would benefit my career, and also because I needed something to keep me connected to God. I wanted to know why my child had to die. I sat out that fall semester, but I started again that same winter. That fall, I learned the meaning of Isaiah 55:8, "For my thoughts are not your thoughts, neither are your ways my ways," declares the Lord. For example, my very first class upon my return to the Sword of the Spirit Bible Institute (SSBI) was Homiletics I (the art of writing and preaching sermons). The curriculum during that time was Homiletics I–IV.

My SSBI's founder and homiletics professor had the reputation of being the hardest professor of all. I've seen grown men crumble and question their call to the pulpit-preaching ministry under his tutelage. To further add to my despair I was the ONLY non-preacher in his class. My pastor required all leaders in his church to attend formal biblical training classes. The school is accredited, and we were an extension of the Richmond Virginia Seminary in Richmond Virginia (where I received my Bachelor's of Science degree in theology). That said, all lay people (non-preachers) earning a B.A. had to enroll in homiletics, but this time I was all by myself with pastors from other established churches and their ministerial understudies.

I knew from the start that this didn't look good, especially not for me, because I was still in emotional pain from losing Asia. I really was doing all I could to keep from screaming at the top of my lungs every morning when I woke up.

The first day he announced, "As seriously as you take this class, that is as serious as you will take your ministry."

I thought to myself, "What ministry? My child is dead, I don't have a ministry, and God certainly isn't interested in using me for anything."

Read the Text!

Next he stated, "Noah built an ark that floated because he followed instructions. Do not procrastinate. One day you will meet the bear, and you will either eat the bear or the bear will eat you. Never get to the point where you think you have it made. The theme of this class is *Read the text, Read the text, Read the Text!!*"

This presented a challenge to me. Being a sports fan and having a competitive nature, my professor's words, even though I was confused by them, seemed to be challenging me. Maybe fighting this "bear" would answer some of the questions I was wrestling with. I looked at his reference to fighting the bear as being similar to the account in Genesis 32:22–32, in which Jacob wrestles with the angel all night until the angel finally blessed him.

I had a hole in my heart, and if I wrestled with this fictitious bear my professor was talking about maybe I, too, would be blessed. I knew it wouldn't bring Asia back, but maybe I could mend my broken heart and go on with life. In hindsight I recall Homiletics I–IV as being my favorite classes. Little did I realize that this was God's restoration and healing in me.

He was healing me and I was learning how to worship and love Him again. The first writing assignment (I wouldn't dare call them sermons or sermonettes) was to write about Luke 19:28–31, which is the story of Jesus needing a donkey to ride on and sending the disciples into town to get a donkey that no one had ever ridden on before. The Master was in need of a donkey, so the disciples took one from a total stranger and brought it to Him. It was in the researching and writing of my first homework assignment that I began to get answers to some of my most burning questions. The next week, when I was reading my paper aloud during class, tears streamed down my face.

I remember saying, "Oh Lord, why did my child have to die?"

I sensed His voice ever so sweetly. "She is my child too and I will bring good out of her death."

Why Me?

I kept coming back to the question of, *Why me?* Why did He allow this to happen to me? I was worshipping God. I was taking the kids to church. Clifton had such a heart for the inner city. We opened up our home to feed kids who didn't have enough to eat; we bought school supplies and uniforms for the others who couldn't afford them. We were doing what we were supposed to be doing. And yet, God allowed this to happen. It didn't add up. People say you can't ask God why He does what He does, but I say, "Why not? If He is my Father, why can't I ask Him why?" So I did.

I remember distinctly my grandmother telling me as a child to "be careful what you ask for—you might get it."

Well I wanted to know from God why He let Asia die, to which I sensed Him reply. "I gave my Son for you."

I was so angry with His response that I never again asked God why Asia had to die. In fact, after that response, I tried to move as far away from God as I could. The pain I felt was so great that I couldn't bring myself to continuously pursue this all-loving God. How could He be so cruel, how could Asia's death be for His use or be part of some bigger plan? But deep down in my soul I understood exactly what giving His Son for me meant.

When God Doesn't Comfort

As Christians, we are *supposed* to understand

God's Word, and it is *supposed* to give you comfort in all situations. But what if it doesn't do that? One of the biggest joys in my life was gone, and I just wanted the world to end. But I couldn't give in to my emotions. Besides, Clifton, and especially Isiah, needed me.

I continued going through the motions of what I was supposed to do every day, whether I felt like it or not. I continued to lift my hands during praise and worship, say hallelujah and participate in the service, even though I felt like I was no longer able to "worship in spirit and in truth" because my truth was grief, loss, and pain. Nevertheless, I continued to attend church and continued to love my neighbor as myself. To me this was another step in my healing—getting back to some kind of routine, what felt "normal" to me. Even though I felt like I couldn't worship, I asked others to worship for me. This was another step in my healing, asking others to do what I couldn't do.

Subsequently on my journey to healing and in search of ways to go on, I pursued my master's degree in counseling. This was a tremendous leap forward in the healing process for both my husband and me. The saying, "Physician, heal thyself," was one I took to heart.

When I entered the bereavement course curriculum I was drawn in like a moth to a flame. I began to understand the feelings and emotions I was experiencing and started to understand what my family was enduring as well. Many people go through life believing that they don't need counseling. We can all benefit from being led into our own truth. The truth for us was that Asia died and she was not coming back. We are still here, and we must go on through this life without her.

Asia SiVon Cottom Memorial Scholarship Fund

It was also during that time that Clifton and I expanded on the Asia SiVon Cottom Memorial Scholarship Fund to include accepting applications from upper classmen. This was a huge step forward in our healing journey. It was our personal story of going from tragedy to triumph. It was so rewarding, and still is, to bring goodness to the lives of others.

I guess you could say that I remained faithful in my actions, even though my heart was far from God. This was another step in my healing—facing my painful emotions and doing what I needed to do. We wanted to do something significant with Asia's legacy, to have something beautiful come out of our pain.

CHAPTER TWENTY-SEVEN

The Story of Job

Notes for Grief and Bereavement Counseling

Thanatology is the study of the effects of death and dying.

Three major aspects are:

1. Social – meaning common, shared, or collective
2. Psychological – the way/how a person dies or leaves
3. Spiritual – "The Comforter is always with you"

When offering counseling services, we must start from where the person is currently at in his/her journey. The timeline for healing and processing is highly individual. Children grieve differently than adults, and their grief period largely depends on the actions of the adults. Sometimes a loss can be complicated by other factors, such as multiple deaths or unresolved grief.

One must deal with the loss of certain dreams or aspirations one has had. The loss may change one's responsibilities in life. Grief is a normal response to the loss of any significant person, object, or opportunity.

Elisabeth Kübler Ross: Stages of Grief

Although not everyone will follow the same order in Elisabeth Kübler Ross's stages, each one of us will go through these stages of grief every time we experience a substantial loss.

- Denial/shock
- Anger
- Bargaining/guilt
- Depression
- Acceptance

The Book of Job

Whenever clergy or another religious person talks to you about your suffering, they may tell you to read the book of Job. Even if you aren't a religious person, you can still glean truths from this time-honored story. The wisdom in this classic book in Scripture is useful for the Christian and non-Christian alike.

Here is a synopsis:

The story of Job is one of the oldest stories of the Scriptures. One of the issues it tackles is the never-ending question, "Why do bad things happen to good people?" In this book, the stage is set as Satan requests permission to afflict and test Job in his effort to prove that, given the right circumstances, the righteous cannot remain faithful. In the divine allowance of God, the devil attacks the life of Job on many different occasions in his attempt to see failure in man's dependence upon God. His three friends came to him and tried to offer comfort in his time of need. They were silent for seven days, and they commiserated with Job by tearing their robes in grief. This was helpful to Job, because he knew they felt empathy for him. However, after seven days they started to speak, and what they said brought more harm than good. The message they gave was clear: "You must have done something to deserve this." All the advice they gave Job was erroneous. Even Job's wife told him to curse God and die. She didn't say this to hurt him further; in fact, she said this because she saw how much he was suffering day in and day out, and she felt his pain. She truly thought the only way to relieve this agony was for him to die. The book of Job records both his thoughts and his responses to his friends when they tried to make sense of all Job's suffering. Their assumptions of the "whys" of hardship and even misguided advice are sprinkled throughout the counsel of the friends. The dialogue shows the anguish and despair of Job. The fight for faithfulness continues throughout the story.

Job's conversation with God and His reply are also part of this record. When Job is truly fed up with all the agony the Lord has given him, he retaliates with anger directed at God. God completely puts him in his place by giving Job a list of things that only God can do and control. Who is man to question him? Job is remorseful for his anger, confesses that he spoke of things he did not understand, and repents before God. In the conclusion of the story, Satan is defeated and God declares a victory for the person of faith who chooses to serve God. A miracle of restoration and provision is the reward to Job as God blesses Job in such a way that they become the greatest years of his life. In closing, Job wrestled with the adversary, but God showed Himself faithful.

Michelle's Experience with Job

Reading Job isn't an instant fix, however. As Michelle says, "Every time I read Job, it affected me differently, but it didn't give me comfort or resolution until recently." She explains:

First of all, I couldn't really identify with Job because he was considered by God to be a completely upright person. While yes, I was certainly trying to be faithful, I didn't consider myself to be a perfect person. Secondly, Job's reward in the end, which was "double for your trouble," offered me no comfort. Through the lawsuit launched against American Airlines, we received a monetary settlement. Yes, it was a blessing, but it would never make up for the loss of our child. And I would dare say that Job would have felt this way; loss of a child is something that stays with you your entire life.

Although the book of Job wasn't helping me, I continued—as my professor had advised—to "Read the text, read the text, read the text." I kept thinking that maybe I was missing something; maybe there were deeper, more profound answers to why people suffer. I must have read the book over twenty times in the last thirteen years.

In the meantime, I was still living my own Job story. In the years that followed Asia's death, trial after trial came: the deaths of family members and friends from the stress; people grieving all around me whom *I* was trying to comfort; the media hounding us; conspiracy theories swirling around; negative press about us benefitting financially from Asia's death. The list goes on.

Until you live your own Job story, you may never see what it is trying to tell you. Everyone has to go through his/her own steps of grieving to come to a place of acceptance before the healing process can begin. And those steps are different for everyone.

Sometimes when I read the Book of Job I laugh because I see that his friends are typical and hilarious. They told Job what to do, and they were all wrong. Even his wife tells him to curse God and die. For those of you who have a friend who is grieving over a loss please do not be a "Job's friend."

Some of the "wrong" things typical "Job's folks" have said to Clifton and me include:

- "Oh, your daughter died in 9/11? Well on that day I was ..." *They say this before they listen to anything we have to say. We don't care if you were watching it on TV in Walmart.*

- "My brother was in the Pentagon, but he lived." *We're glad to hear that, but how is that supposed to comfort us?*

- "Can I ask you a personal question? Did you get any of her body back?" *This is a very painful issue for us. If you have to ask whether you can ask a personal question, then more likely than not, the answer is that you shouldn't.*

- "Well at least you have another child." *Is this supposed to comfort us?*

- "The Lord giveth, and the Lord taketh away." *Really? Why are you telling us that? It's nowhere in the Bible, anyway.*

- "You can have more kids." *No one will replace Asia.*

- "Well, she was only eleven." *What does that even mean?*

- "Why did you let her go on the trip?" or, "Why did you let her go by herself?" *This was a school trip. It was perfectly normal that she would go with her teacher. Are you trying to make us feel worse?*

- "You are not over that yet?" *No, and I never will be. Talk to me when you lose a child.*

- "I lost my mother at ninety-six years of age, so I know what you're going through." *I don't think you do.*

Please, I beg you, be a good and patient friend to those who have suffered loss. Share your hugs; offer a shoulder to lean on; but please remember that the less you say often is the best thing you can say.

I'm a reader, and it takes me about two days to read the book of Job, when I read it as if I were trying to quench an insatiable thirst. Each time I started reading the book, I would say that *this time* I would get something out of the story. Yet, it still didn't make sense. However, the book did make me yearn for God again and realize that He is sovereign; and because He is who He is, He can do whatever He wants to do and I can learn to go on.

Learning to Understand

I would talk to God just like I talk to anyone I wanted to share my heart and soul with. I didn't volunteer for this, and I certainly didn't sign up to carry the grief that followed. "Of all the people in the world, why did you give this burden to us?" I would say to Him. And if I dared voice these questions to others, some would say dumb stuff like, "Oh, you can handle it," or "You are supposed to reach the masses." My question to them has always been, "How do you know that?" Of all the people in this world, couldn't God choose someone else to be in the forefront, someone stronger, better equipped?

Some people would tell us that the reason we went through our tragedy lies in the scholarship fund we started. This insinuates that God forced us down a grievous path and caused indescribable suffering in our lives so that others could benefit. If this were the case, then God would be a sadist. To those individuals I say, "Couldn't He, in all His wisdom and might, come up with an easier and less painful way to educate these youth?"

The Bible says, "For my thoughts are not your thoughts, nor are your ways my ways, says the Lord" (Isaiah 55:8). But if starting the scholarship fund was the reason Asia died, then surely He could have shared His "thoughts" with us in other ways.

After reading through the book of Job for at least the twentieth time, I still cannot make sense of it. And that's okay; I've learned things by reading it that have pointed me back to God, back to His loving arms, and that is the place I need to be. Yes, the circumstances and the events of Job's life are baffling if we try to fully understand them. But perhaps we don't need to make sense of it; that is not the ultimate goal. Perhaps the ultimate goal is to remain faithful, "to do justly, to love mercy, and to walk humbly with our God" (Micah 6:8). God restores us after our obedience, even if we don't understand what in the world is going on!

As the years passed after Asia's death, the struggles inside me, and the emotional pain I was experiencing on a daily basis, were driving me further away from God. However, even though I didn't want to hear what He had to say, I couldn't get away from Him. The further I tried to push Him away, the closer He drew to me. When I couldn't "stand up," I knew He was carrying me. I felt like I was on a merry-go-round; I was letting go of God, but He kept pulling me back on. He simply would not let me go. When I finally came to grips with this, when I realized He was with me every moment of every day, when I finally began to rest in this fact, I truly began to heal.

As Christians, what you are taught depends on the denomination you come from. In my case, God was teaching me in real life who He really is. I could come to Him with anything, including being angry with Him. I needed to admit that I was furious with God. I needed to share all of my emotions and thoughts with Him—good and bad.

Because I am a worshipper at heart when I wake up in the early morning, at around 4:00 or 5:00 a.m., I talk with God before my feet hit the floor. During my times of grieving, I would start out by pouring my emotions out to God, then eventually I would work my way around to a song or something else that drew me into His presence.

Today, I can say "Good morning, Holy Spirit. Command my day." Think about that—even though I don't have the answers as to why He chose my family and me to live this way, my relationship with God has deepened in ways I could never imagine. That is just me. For others, the healing process means other things. And that's okay.

CHAPTER TWENTY-EIGHT

Flying on New Wings

"We all needed to find our new wings to fly again, and we all did it in our own way."

We don't have any control over the tragedies in life. We don't choose when, where, or how they come. This is reality. And acceptance means reality. The Cottoms have come to the place where they've accepted that they can't change what happened, and they have to learn to live with the here and now. *Not* accepting means to continue living in denial, to continue to live with pain and bitterness. It means never loving again. Perhaps it means retaliating against people who had nothing to do with the tragedy they and others have gone through. And that's certainly not what the Cottoms want to do.

"I choose to go on, to accept what God allows—even though there are times that I still become sad and my eyes fill with tears when I think about the times Asia and I will never share," Michelle said.

Loss of any kind brings pain. Your pain may not be the same as the pain the Cottoms experience, but we all need healing from what we've gone through. We all need to come to a place of acceptance, of being able to work through our emotional trauma, and to do so according to who we are and the way we were made. This path is unique for all of us, and we cannot expect others to be where we "think" they should be. It doesn't really matter how peace comes, what matters is that it does come. The Cottoms are living proof of this.

Although God works in different ways with different people, regardless of their faith, one overarching commonality is the overwhelming sense of God's love and care. We are not alone in this hostile world. This is the reality. If we run to God, not away from Him, then His love slowly, but steadily, becomes a reality to us. Michelle and Clifton have received God's love and His embrace, and are able to impart it to others.

As Michelle has said, "We all needed to find our new wings to fly again, and we all did it in our own way."

Clifton's journey to self-healing was to first learn to cry in public, with his wife and with others, to cry and release it that way. He bottled it up for so many years, and when he was able to let it go, he felt so much better. He says that every time he talks about Asia's passing he heals a little. Every time he is with a friend who is pure in heart, he heals a little. Every time he helps one of the youths in his charge, he heals a little. Every time he is able to act like a substitute dad to kids without fathers, or to his god-children, he heals a little.

Clifton is living the life of giving back to the world even though so much was taken from him. Sometimes he claims it is his faith that has pulled him along, and sometimes he still just does the right thing, despite his doubts at the time. He is a true man, and a true believer.

Isiah often felt as if he didn't fit in anywhere. Asia helped him to feel good about himself; she taught him self-confidence and how to do things. He misses her in his daily life, just as they all do. Part of his healing has come with time, part of it has come through his being faithful and continuing his active church life, and a large part of it has come through his writing and his music. He has never stopped praying since that first day of the tragedy when he dropped to his knees. He has a personal relationship with God.

Bishop Ross was able to empathize to the deepest levels of compassion. In many ways he suffered through all of this just as the Cottoms did. He didn't come at them with things they were supposed to believe, or things they should be doing, but he walked beside them through all of this.

Bishop Ross helped Clifton by giving him the Youth Ministry in the church. He trusted him enough to do that. Bishop Ross allowed Clifton the freedom to worship in a different church. Usually a family is supposed to be together on Sunday mornings, but Bishop Ross said, "Wherever you can be healed, wherever you can grow, that is where you need to be." Clifton needed something different than Michelle. There are so many more men his age in Pastor Jackson's congregation. So, that's where he needed to be. Isiah and his mother join Clifton at Pastor Jackson's church for the Saturday services.

Pastor Jackson's journey led him to share the steps necessary for healing. The first step is that we must recognize we are in need of healing. This may already be a stumbling block for a number of people. Many of us are too proud or too afraid to admit it. The second step is to put ourselves in a place where we can heal—not just the physical environment, but also in surrounding ourselves with people who can help us.

Pastor Jackson took his own road to healing as well. Yes, he suffered under the pressure of all the stress in the aftermath of 9/11. His body broke down, and he couldn't take it any longer. But, he still managed to get back to a place of healing. He didn't have the right people around him to help him; there were some, but not enough, to feel safe and to feel that release. But now Pastor Jackson is able to teach about God's healing and His love because he crawled through the valley of pain.

When something happens to us and we have no control over it, we must allow a power greater than ourselves to show us how to go on. There is no recipe for how to do it. There's no right or wrong. We don't have to like the circumstances, but in order to go on we must ultimately come to the place of acceptance.

Epilogue

Asia received her new wings when she went to heaven but we needed new wings to fly again. We couldn't find them. It took us thirteen years to find the peace and healing that eluded us for so long after we lost our daughter. *His* peace. *His* healing. We are finally beginning to feel the wind under our wings again.

Even though we still don't like it that we lost our daughter—and we don't think that anyone comes to the place of "liking" their loss; but we have accepted it. Because we have accepted it, we have been healed from the extreme pain and the sting of her death. We have been freed from the grief in our day-to-day lives. As in the Job story, God has restored some of the positives in our lives. That doesn't mean that we don't miss her or ache to hold her again, but we can still walk, talk, breathe, and have fun. We can still love our family, friends, neighbors, and our fellow man. And most importantly, we can still love God.

We are free to go on.

Clifton and Michelle Cottom

About the Authors

Clifton A. Cottom is an educational paraprofessional with twenty-nine years of extensive public school, group and private home experience with inner city children, including those with developmental delays. For the past fifteen years, he has served in increasingly responsible leadership positions in the District of Columbia Public School System. Mr. Cottom assists leadership in critical efforts to rebrand, rebuild, and revitalize schools by helping students become change agents in their community and the world at large. Subsequently, he serves as an expert in the area of behavior management in crisis situations, using his in-depth knowledge of behavior management techniques.

Mr. Cottom works closely with children and adults, and he is an expert in interpreting and relaying information from books and periodicals. He assists students with preparing academic papers and tutors adults in mathematics (his strong suit). Clifton is a strong leader who recognizes, develops, and utilizes the strengths and talents of individuals to build highly successful teams. He has been recognized for his exceptional accomplishments with awards and certificates of appreciation.

Mr. Cottom was born and raised in Washington, D.C. His desire is to tell Asia's story so that her legacy has a profound effect on all of us.

Michelle A. Cottom Ph.D. has enjoyed an extensive career, spanning two decades, in civil rights, human rights, equal employment opportunity, policy development, dispute resolution, and program evaluation. Dr. Cottom is a Supervisory EEO Manager in the federal government. Throughout her career, Dr. Cottom has served as a sought after advisor and expert in affirmative employment, alternative dispute resolution and federal sector complaints processing. Her proven passion for transforming underperforming civil rights programs, establishing leading programs in the areas of equal employment opportunity and civil rights, and delivering proper customer service has yielded tangible results for the federal agencies with which she has worked.

Dr. Cottom is a Veteran of the United States Army. Her experience there yielded her the self-discipline, initiative, confidence and intelligence that became the hallmark of her federal career. She is a strong proponent of Communities and Civil Rights and has been a disability advocate since 1984.

Dr. Michelle A. Cottom was born in Washington, D.C., and raised in Elyria, Ohio. After living and working in several areas of the U.S. and abroad, she eventually settled in her old stomping grounds. This is where she met and married Mr. Cottom. The Cottoms currently reside in Prince George's County Maryland and have one adult son, Isiah.

Clifton A. Cottom

Mr. Cottom is a proud graduate of Spingarn Senior High School and his educational career includes his studies at Catonsville Community College and the University of Minnesota.

Mr. Cottom has received numerous notable awards including, Basketball Coach of the Year for both middle and high school, Community recognition from a nationally syndicated radio program (Tom Joyner Morning Show) "Real Fathers, Real Men" Award and "A Spiritual Father and a Real Man" Award from the Youth Ministry of his church and many other Certificates and Letters of Appreciation.

Michelle A. Cottom, Ph.D.

Dr. Cottom holds a Bachelor's of Science Degree in Theology, a Master's of Arts Degree in Counseling, and a Ph.D. in Divinity/Christian Ministry.

Dr. Cottom is an active member of community groups such as Blacks in Government (BIG), Federally Employed Women (FEW), Executive Women in Government (EWG), and National Association of Professional Women (NAPAW).Together, Clifton and Michelle Cottom are co-founders of the Asia SiVon Cottom (ASC) Memorial Scholarship Fund, and sit on the Fund's executive board.